MW01277946

Decalogue
ten Ottawa poets

Decalogue
ten Ottawa poets

edited by
rob mclennan

Ottawa 2006

Decalogue: ten Ottawa Poets
© 2006, the authors

cover design - Tanya Sprowl
cover artwork - "Nuns vs. Dragons" by Bhat Boy
designed by Cheryl Mayhew and Jennifer Mulligan
edited for the press by rob mclennan

printed and bound in Canada
by Custom Printers, Renfrew, Ontario

Chaudiere Books
858 Somerset Street West
Main Floor
Ottawa, Ontario
K1R 6R7

www.chaudierebooks.com
email: info@chaudierebooks.com

Library and Archives Canada Cataloguing in Publication

Decalogue : ten Ottawa poets / edited by Rob McLennan.

Poems.
ISBN-13: 978-0-9781601-3-5
ISBN-10: 0-9781601-3-4

I. McLennan, Rob, 1970-

PS8295.7.O8D43 2006   C811'.6   C2006-906843-7

Decalogue: ten Ottawa poets

Bill McGillivray's Cap

Stephen Brockwell

Stephen Brockwell spent the first half of his life in Montreal, and the second half in Ottawa. Where he will spend the third half is uncertain. His poetry collections include *The Wire in Fences* (Toronto ON: Balmuir Publishing, 1988), *The Cometology* (Toronto ON: ECW Press, 2001) and *Fruitfly Geographic* (ECW Press, 2004), which won the Archibald Lampman Award.

Scarecrow

You want to tell the cane-swinging codger
to get off the plywood in your back yard
and find trash of his own to fall down on,
but in this neighbourhood the arteries
clog with identical mansard-roofed red
brick houses, identical driveways cracked
by the relentless crush and stretch of freeze and thaw,
blue carbon copy hydrants on the south
side of the street, street lights that perfect eyes
could not distinguish. You stoop to lift him
while his daughter apologizes with
such humility you'd think falling on
someone else's trash was a kind of theft.
And your thoughts turn, like a crow in flight,
to his surprising weight, say, four twenty-
kilo sacks of P.E.I. potatoes
stitched with enormous skill into the shape
of an old man, a monument for some
forgotten autumn festival, or prop
for the Halloween play at an abandoned school.
It's at that moment you begin to fear,
"This may be me in another forty years,
wetting my pants in someone else's yard,
failing to grip with my cane the discarded
plywood from a neighbour's renovations,
unable to recall my daughter's name,
flailing for my woollen cap to cover
the white relics of my remaining hairs,
groping for glasses that could never fall
from my broad fat nose, demanding to know
why I'm propped up by a stranger. Give me
this old man's humour and his wit; let me
curse the taxi driver and the barman."

Bill McGillivray's Cap

I may not yet be fifty but the field
underneath this cap's not growing taller.
I can't imagine going to the barn
without it. Someone would have to sneak
into the shed and steal it from the nail
it's hung on since Dad brought it home for me
from Illinois before I'd forget to
put it on or take it off. If it weren't there?
I'd stand as dumb as a November field.
I've had this John Deere cap near thirty years.
It wasn't the last thing he brought me home.
It was the only thing he brought me home.

Karikura and a Loaf of Bread

Karikura came to me and asked for bread.
I said, "Karikura, I have ten dollars. Take it
and buy yourself a decent breakfast."
Karikura scolded me, "I do not want your money.
I asked you for bread because the bread you make
is not very good. If you do not make more,
you will never make a loaf that anyone will eat."

Peter's Complete Shakespeare

I cherish it. She gave me the book, back
long before I knew I appreciated
literature. I was a bit of a fake.
It was faux appreciation. I wanted
to be fancy. I often pick it up
and thumb through it. Someone had interspersed
little notes here and there throughout the book,
brief, hand-scribbled character descriptions.
Every once in a while I'll thumb through it
and find one of the notes and open it;
it's as if I've found it for the first time.
Whoever owned the book was smart enough,
or thought enough of the book, not to write
in the margins. The onionskin pages
deteriorated just enough to see
the old engravings underneath. Often
I've worried that I haven't taken good
care of it. It sits on a bookshelf, right.

Hammer

Horseshoe, coat rack, toy box, fence, house, stall—
what isn't put together with a hammer?
Every family has one in the cellar,
hanging from a hook on a concrete wall
or lodged at the bottom of a box of tools.
If you haven't shed a blackened nail or sucked
on a swollen thumb your hammer struck,
go fix a creaking plank or hang a picture.
Look at this simple thing: a lump of steel
wedged with a shim to a hardwood handle
shaped to drive a nail with a few hard blows.
Some say the Romans cast a long shadow
with the short handle of a hammer.
Don't blame the soldier or the carpenter.

Mark Bradley's Wife

Can I pick my wife? She's the finest
woman a man could find. Loving, sweet, warm
in bed—oh, come on now, baby, I mean
comfortable to sleep with; you know that—
I guess I'm doing laundry for a week.
It's true. Other women demand too much:
remodel the kitchen, fix this, paint that.
Others love you for who you are and give.
Terri taught me to give by giving herself.
A lesson her mother said this redneck
bastard couldn't learn. When Philip turned three,
Terri had been working at Walmart for—
What was it, honey, five years? You worked hard.
No one puts more into her work than you do.
Philip developed asthma and she missed
too many shifts taking him to hospital
until we had him diagnosed. I still
hear his breathing. Huuggh huuggh.
[Difficult to transcribe wheezing in throat.]
You has us scared boy, eh, Philip? Laid off!
They pink slipped the most beautiful woman
you've ever seen in a pink slip. Came home
crying, weeping, and I just held her.
Believe it or not, I said not one word.

The Last Eloquence of Uncle John

An orifice is a kind affliction
all relief and infection leave and enter. It is a door
revolving until our final breath or defecation—
but of that enough, for let me speak
of the baby for whom all are pleasure:
its, its mother's, its father's.
The poor dog has had a few explored.
Of the pleasure older children take
aunt Rose would have me embarrassed to speak,
but of an old man's keen nostril
and of the exuberance of my digestion
I can speak until my lungs forget to breathe.

Joanne's Nissan Altima

A Japanese car beats a man for warmth
and reliability, don't you think?
Everyone falls in love with their first car.
Or do we love the cars we can't afford?
I read that German men with BMWs
have more sex. They didn't survey women.
I'd like someone to explain that to me.
The whole car-buying process is like mating.
Did I say mating? Dating, I meant dating.
We shop around for a model we wouldn't
be embarrassed to be seen with. You look
for evidence that we'll give good mileage.
I'm sorry. I love my car. I bought it
five years ago and it's cost me little more
than oil changes, brakes and monthly payments.
It brought me home safely through a blizzard,
back up to North Bay after I dumped Paul.

Sorus

The fiddlehead, silent mimic,
balances the taste of butter

on the tongue with the delicate
palate of an unfurling fern.

The sorus, I'm told, trellises spores
that cling like fruit to the frond.

Roving the forest for deer, boar
and such large game, the Saxon

must have lacked the Latin ear
for minutiae that would give

the tongue a name for this
tiny heap of fertile green.

Karikura's Fiddle

When Karikura played fiddle and sang,
you thought the day would end in sunrise.
We loved to hear one Karikura song:
> *Bee lem ah la*
> *Ee nay gó la*
> *Bee lem ah la*
> *Ee nay gó la*
> *Hamari o no la ma*
> *No goro o h'mo Allah*

I asked Karikura the meaning of the words.
Karikura said, "The first verse means,
'My goats are gone.' The second verse,
'There is no grass left.' These are repeated.
The third verse means, 'I too may have to go.'
And the final verse, 'Thank God for my fiddle.'"

Ingredients for Certain Poems by Al Purdy

Wild Ameliasburgh grapes
        crushed by two hundred pounds of fifty-year-old Al
wild Penticton yeast
        from apple boughs and vines
        from the old man's feet
imparting more fragrant fruit
        than any brewer's yeast a poet might buy
Roblin Lake water with a hint of mercury
        and fourstroke fuel
        unremarked like any minor hazard of the 1970s
a carboy with a rubber stopper
the sickness of poems
sickness of scenery
he will never say a word about

Cachel, Roblin Mills, Belleville
        villages of recent early history
        strung together by
        water from the roots of Algonquin tamarack
        to the leaves of Mont Royal oak
substituting their names for a national mood
        that eludes all but the last rhetoric of lists
        the droning cadences of tavern cusses
        because a man said
I am no man because this is not a country

Ripe, subsidized Saskatchewan barley
        malted in a union shop in Hamilton
ten foot East Kent Goldings
        harvested by the rough hands of Scottish labour,
        compressed into a handful of aromatic pellets
a sachet of dried yeast or
        a tablespoon of breadyeast from a kitchen jar
some wort-filtering device—a sieve, a clean pair of drawers
        a misplaced stocking of Eurithe's
a covered pail in the kitchen
alcoholic tastes for forbidden women
one can't use
developed at great expense

Montréal, Winnipeg, Vancouver
    cities careening into speech
    hammered together with
    iron on the anvil of the Shield
    through fields of maize and barley
    past coulees, cattails and purple loosestrife
homespun whatchamacallits and invasive handles
    coiling themselves under the tongue
    symbionts infecting the language
with the rare disease of an authentic voice

the gift of a wife
with a name even Rocket Richard in his skates
could have wrapped his laces and a song around
the Rocket would have found breath on the bench to sing
    Eurithe, seuls les tendres mots
        m'échappent parfois.
    Lisses sont ton nom et ta peau.
        Ils ne m'échapperont pas.

The fermented applejunk of Bordeaux grape skins
    poured into hand-polished copper stills
half a forest of oak
    split and kiln dried in a warehouse at Nevers,
    strapped into barrels by the Union of French Coopers
a stone walled cellar under a dilapidated chateau
    where booze can age in the damp for years
water from god knows what European tap or spring
    to dilute it for a simple bottle of imperfect glass
a label chosen for clarity not elegance
the strands of an existence
outside the
never finished sentences

Pangnirtung, Galapagos, L'Anse aux Meadows
    habitations for exotica, sea fringes
    whispered together on a thread of
    air we learned to fly on
    with sandpiper, eider, monarch
monikers no more strange than here for strange places
    where Medusa's children coil their thousand serpents
    turtles bask and dry their shells

and the wapiti gather in vast numbers
not to be named by us but to graze

Fresh peat dried in the rare highland sun
      (at least one bog must entomb a mummified
ancestor of clan Ross
      a patriarch who shambled out of the fog
      and stared up at Aldebaran muttering a Scots drinking song)
Isle of Skye barley threshed by a farmer
      with his eye on profit and a kickback bottle
a hundred times more water than will make it to the cask
      water to steep the grain for germination
water to soak the sweetness from the grist
the strangeness of sediment
from the last bottle
pockets of the human swept into the mainstream

Truva, Samarkand, Plains of Abraham
      sites of text and artifact, parchment and shard
      woven together by the burned black
      ink of scribes and presses, and the black
      blood of blubbering heroes expiring on the sand
It may be that until we write into our history
      the names of three thousand coolie railmakers
      (whose remains the crows and foxes
      scattered across the prairie)
the words of this country will not find us

the gift of a wife
with a name even Bobby Clarke in his box
could be inspired to eloquence by
the boarding bully could be moved by tenderness of sound to sing
      Eurithe, for your name
         I drop my gloves
      not to inflict pain
         but to love

Michelle Desbarats

Drift

Michelle Desbarats is the author of *Last Child to Come Inside* (Ottawa ON: Harbinger / Carleton University Press, 1998) and the chapbook *Eve'n Adam* (Ottawa ON: above/ground press, 1998), later included in *Groundswell: best of above/ground press, 1993-2003* (Fredericton NB: Broken Jaw Press, 2003). She was born in Winnipeg, grew up in Montreal and Charlottetown, and currently resides in Ottawa. Her work has appeared in *Transpoetry*, *Burnt Toast*, *Speak!*, *Meltwater* and on CBC Radio. She was a finalist in the CBC Literary Awards, most recently in 2005. She is working on her second manuscript.

Imprint

how love first appeared
what clothes it borrowed
the color it chose for its hair
will always call you
even later

someone standing there
with nothing for you
but a pale blue shirt
and the way it hangs
calling

the first heart
you grew for it

All Night It Has Been Sleeping With You

It doesn't always but last night
the day came upstairs,
you are always amazed at
how much it sounds just like
a cat when it walks,
and found a place near your
feet to sleep.
During the night, the day
moved around,
once it was stretched
across the
width of the bed
like a horizon
and once
light twitched among the
day's folds as though
it were dreaming.
You don't always spend the
night with the day against your legs.
When night comes the day
often finds some little
place to curl into -
a hollow perhaps, from where
if it wants,
it can see the stars
and because of this
you don't often get to see
how the day begins
before orange sunrise blues it,
when it is
still and quiet
enough to hear the
birds begin to sing in
that first light
pearling from its small fangs.

Just Once

Just once it's okay to
pack, follow someone else's dream
because there's a chance
that hidden in other than your own
is something. Try this if you've
tried everything and sitting in the diner of
someone else's dream, you could
be handed a menu out of which
you can order anything.

Waiting

What people do to pass the time
between when things happen of account,
those long lonely nights and
the hands must do something
with sharp instruments onto
surfaces; incise micro-thin lines
called decoration that recount
tales of past adventure.
Beneath only the light of stars, maybe a
moon, expanses used to
lay down history and then
the night's ink rubbed in
so while they sleep you can read
what you've drawn and see
the great ships again, the vast
whales and oceans,
then leave
for others to find and polish
your scrimshaw people.

Saturday Morning Re-entry

Some people wake up between
the sky and the earth some people wake
up too soon there are
times that should be gone through
while still asleep breathing that
kind of oxygen some people
wake in their beds, get up to breakfast
but some wake too soon for
a Saturday morning and find the blue stuff
still below them
and the earth so close too far to
jump to but just a fall toward some
people wake up still bound within
the metal of their last dreams, hoping praying
what could carry them through the night
can get them through the day some
people wake up and holding cups of coffee they
decide this time they'll make the effort to
step out onto the porch and watch the shuttle's
bullet path across the sky
coming home, what returning home looks like,
how the heart arrives first
and the body following,
bright dot against the blue, some people wake too
early on a Saturday morning, their bodies
still miles away and something breaks up high
over Texas, leaving a trail of parts.

In the New Kitchen

When Eve handed the apple, warm from
her teeth, to Adam
he said after, that he had felt coerced and
that there were two places where he
could have stopped everything and he'd
known it then. So that now in this strewn
place, if he thought of it at all, it was as
something that never should have happened. She
would ask him, her voice delicate as
small branches, to talk about, at least, the taste
for there had only been the one -
no bright fruit now in this beige land.
But he would only say it
shouldn't have been and then look at her darkly.
So she would detach herself from
the teaming of animals around her still trying
to find homes for themselves and walk
up a little rise. She would remember
how it broke away in her mouth like the snap of a day.
She would keep
such skin alive, burnishing memory with her robe.
And everyday she went out looking, for
what she did not know; perhaps the dark companion
of a seed.
But she knew the last part. How, when she found
it, she would dig with a stone into the ground and
bury it. They'd all been tossed out, her, Adam,
the animals. The gate had been closed by an angel
with a burning sword. Then all that had
disappeared. She'd watched two snails
slide away on the new floor to where must lie the sea.
She'd watched two birds rise up toward the
direction of sky. She knew she was going
to be blamed for everything - the jagged
trees on the horizon, the hills mauve with distance.

Celery Dish

When all was ready
it was the passage of the
sharp cut celery in the long crystal
dish that my grandmother
placed in my smaller hands to
carry from the steamed
kitchen into the
linen and candled dining room
jeweled with the heat of silver
covered bowls of vegetables and scented
with cooked meat.
Her words dusted soft from a thousand
floured pie crusts, tempered
by heat, be careful now,
as the weight of the cooled glass
passed from her into me
and the way fraught with
worn and polished linoleum,
patterned carpet, different fallings
of light, the murmur of voices,
and my wonder of whether
I could, once again, complete
the journey
that begins everything.

If

If you don't know what something
eats, try feeding it anything and
see if it starts to die.

Drift

Drift, said the day
as I began it in my usual
frenzy,
it placed its clear as air
hands on my small ones
where again I'd taken
up the oars.
The wood stilled
and water
dripped from the sharp horizontaled
edges and things quieted.
It was then I felt
the day move
beneath me
the deep
and sealed machinery of the day
moving everything
as my hands would have
and curiosity beginning
in me of where the day might take me
that I might not
take myself.
And then, at my shoulder,
the mountain appearing
that I always meant to climb,
with the little house at its peak
that, at night, looked
like a star among the stars,
and the path
leading up to it, to where
I'd meant to stand.
This mountain, this house,
that I'd thought were but two of
the precious things I'd had to
leave behind,
here again as though having
never left my side.

Plummeting

Anita Dolman

Born in southwestern Ontario, **Anita Dolman** is a poet, freelance writer and editor. Her work has appeared in *Grain Magazine, Geist, Utne, The Fiddlehead, Latchkey.net, Prism International, ottawater* (*www.ottawater.com*), *The Antigonish Review,* as well as various other publications, including her first chapbook, *Scalpel, tea and shot glass* (Ottawa ON: above/ground press, 2004). She gratefully acknowledges the financial support of the City of Ottawa.

Family comes ashore

They'll share the memory of a ship
churning against bottomless black,
the wooden beds creaking, dry bones
echoing through the rusty hull;
empty sky rattling its wind against the deck.

Seasick
                    a young mother vomits sticky fluid into a mop pail.
        A young father leaves for the top deck,
has two children to feed,
a new language to learn.

One deck above there is dancing.

On the floor by their mother's bed,
the two girls gather their hands
from their dress pockets,
pile new pennies into a shallow mound in the dust,
count again to 30. How many of these
will Canadian liquorice cost?

In Hamilton, on Pitt Street, their crate arrives. The father racks the boards
with a borrowed crowbar from an Irish mechanic.
Polish housewives, fat with the conceit of earlier arrival,
roll their thick stomachs over the balcony rails
and watch each item as it's extracted; shopping.

The young family does not know this yet;
       will learn it in the coming cold
              with the sudden absence of dolls and cutlery.

For now their small faith has been placed in the placating tones/
       of immigration officials
who tell them it will still be okay, that there are other jobs to be had,
as they struggle to ignore the dark smells
wafting from the factories around the dying lake.

Image

Still as the canvas, motionless, eyes on the tourists
who pass by, or stare at her
through the deep glass,
wait, impossibly,
for her to dance,
smile,
move
the delicate lines of her small, ivory gown,
perfected wisps and laces, lush, little-girl lashes and lips,
the details for which, at age six, he chose her.

Still sitting still,
there have been decades
when it was too much to bear,
her oils turning to salt
one particle at a time,
the students copying her over
and over in charcoal,
pencil,
pastels.

If her beauty could will it,
she'd bend the gold-leaf frame
that time moulded around her.
Her big brown eyes have been everything,
but no reward can be enough for this.
She would kick the lazy professor
from his swollen leather chair at the door,
who says "overly sentimental,"
"hardly worth all the fuss;"
kick him hard, in the shins,

if she could get the fuck out.

Directions

The heels of my shoes click louder
such a pretty city,
on the cobbles with each wrong turn
the history of architecture flowing
away from the concourse, crossing vast flagstone shadows,
like all the world's rivers into its straaten. Its vast glass facades
now nowhere near the train station, the tourist malls.
hide the absence of buildings bombed out
Three men lean on a brownstone stoop — one old, maybe
in the war, and the war before that one.
60 or not quite; the other two young enough still
The Hague is a museum
to do damage.
rushing to rebuild itself
They watch me carefully, try to learn without words
in fast fashions
whether I speak their tongue or am foreign,/
        fresh from the beaches beyond the city.
over the things that lie beneath.
I keep my map hidden. They cannot decide.
*Step by step, we interpret our differences, the city between us,/
        the distances it might allow.*

Shoes

She tells stories about the war;
the man who hid in their attic that fall,
until the SS found him and the trains took him away
to the work camps, she thinks, but there was no telling
and nothing anyone could have done.

And, of course, there was her cousin, or someone's cousin,
who got his balls blown off, shot clear off, right there in the front yard
and who died, just hours, just minutes or seconds or days later,/
       bled to death,
somewhere around the middle of the war, maybe 1943, sometime
when the schools were closed, which they were then, often.

But not, she thinks, when she fell in the road,
twisting her ankle in the crater by the bridge;
the shell of the bomb lying there, like a target, intact
and she wanting to get closer, to see it, because she was 12
and had never seen one like that, unshattered, just lying in the road.

But the scars, those are from her shoes, too small for growing,
worn and worn, squeezing her toes together, shifting their architecture,/
       so that now,
five decades later, she can't find shoes that fit, that don't crush
the tiny mounds that were once baby toes and now sit shoved up,
eternally raw pink and useless, on top of her feet.

But it was the war then, and who could buy shoes? she says./
       There was so little
and the whole family had scurvy the one year, even the baby, who would
scream and scream and scream, in the dark, in the basement,
in the blackouts, when the bombs fell
and there was so much else to think about.

Cartography

Bolted to the alabaster walls,
great technicolour maps
of oceans and land, lush, frozen,
their landscapes unfolding
through the past,
from Pangaea outward,
Earth's imaginings stretched and folded
into great continents, colliding over time;
Africa wrapped
in the warm, yellow arms
of South America;
to the right the Isle of India;
history creating alliances and enemies,
the eruptions and divisions of change and drift,
until history's cartographers decide,
for a while, to still the inconsolable Earth
with the absolute topography of maps.

I have a deep fear of earthquakes.
At night I dream we are torn apart in a sudden violence,
both of us propelled through miles and millennia
to become our own new lands, separated
by oceans we could not have foreseen.

Haven

There's a motel on the shore,
treed in from view,
and back there, in the shade,
a mother who'll tell me, though not today,
I was conceived in a kitchen,
my life a joke about being bred,
a perpetual discomfort with recipes, domesticity.

Out from the beach the shelf is long,
clear water turning dark in the distance
and I expect the empty drop
each careful motion of my toes over the sand,
my arms spread out, a hydro plane between blues

Until, eventual steps, the distraction of seagulls,
I no longer expect the deep plummet,
snort the blue water in surprise.

After

What remains is the desert,
sand beneath our feet,
and all the world shifting.

Inheritance

Shot glass
      opium pipe
               box
      of fine wood puzzles, carved by hand,
photos to the last;

So much later, every thing
      belies perspective.

Chase

through mildewed aisles
a pudgy boy dodges the rip-traps of the rubber mats
squeaks his sneakers against the black floor
flings his body around the corner shelf
tinned corn tottering   precarious
before settling back into the thick dust
between canned peaches, beans,
soft packs of confectioner's sugar

a pig-tailed girl caroms off the chips display, gains fast,
digs a heal against the cooler
for a launch towards the door,
hands spread towards escape,
pictures the flight over the stoop,   and leaps,
ignores the grocer's call, half-hearted, to
stop, stop that, you kids, you brats,
I've been telling you 32 years;
just once you'd think
you could listen, little bastards

Series

take me
there
now
back
there, the place
somehow
I lost
someone
must know
be able
to say
where it is,
where I left
before we came,
wet with rain,
arriving
on this doorstep —
place I've tried
so hard
but can't
remember
where
and here
we are
again,
re-entering,
stage right
and still
before(
I'm begging you
)before
we begin
again
once more
I'm asking
please
can you
take me
there?

Ontario

Up the road a Pentecostal church
all ripe with lilies against the rocks

The tourist cars slow and swerve on the narrow highway,
unsettled by Mennonite carriages pumping along the shoulder

The drivers hug the median, fearful of so much present history,
but the horses mind their traffic less than flies

And you and I
                         are deep back in the ditch, gathering
          cans, five cents a piece, for candy

The rubber of our boots squeaks against itself,
the marsh cattails arc over our bowed heads

The sun comes up on two, our plastic bags clink heavy;/
          the sound of tin and glass
persuading us to head to town,
collect our earnings.

Wailing wall

All along the western wall
cant rocks the heels of legion to and fro and solemn verse
tips from the rows of dark flowing habits, adjusts the heft
of each man's tread through history, levies
the prayer book's bridge between the Hasid's palms.

The faithful lay their scant belongings
on the path and wait for mercy. Sunlight memorizes
the shadows of their faces
upon the rocks.
In time, the wall comes down,
is rebuilt, comes down again;
the count of days and nights and holy prayers
form just cause in the burnishing of the record.

The land quakes, regenerates;
God tells more parables to the rabbis and novitiates.
Gusts unbroken by surrounding stone
lift the fractured pebbles like dust
and carry them out across the desert.

The offer

                             Fettered
at the edge of the curb
like birds, between Government and Douglas streets,
older than whores should be,
not pretty, not ambitious, not doing this
until something better comes along.

Dark and tangle-haired
she flutters her white leather wings,
zipping, unzipping,
forgetting, remembering
she won't make any money being warm.

Old song, she hollers repeatedly, redundant,
words recorded a younger year;
she flings them now hard and heavy,
half-hearted, at Cadillac windows,
paint of the cars cracked with time.

"Hey, lady, want a date?"
jars me as I lean to the taxi door, opening,
see her, just for a moment
and I am anyone who can pay the fare,
interchangeable as her
before I slide into my seat, close the door.

Fishing

this is the best place to go fishing.
not for the fish, wriggling worms on hooks
bobbing and floating unwatched in shallow water;
barely a creek, snake of slow water sliding
idly into drainage pipe, echoed lapping,
slapping softly against corrugated tin
under the floating dust of occasional flatbeds
quelling birdsong in lags of gravel crunch.

this is the best place to go fishing.
away, but close enough still to hear the tractors,
men steering cattle and lazy machinery
in distant fields, beyond the lulling buzz of dragonflies, heavy bees;
smell of hay and lingering diesel, feel of grass against our backs.

Blindness

Up to you to remember
the details

How many steps
from the path,

Where the doors are,
Where the chair is.

Practice.
        Close your eyes.

Turn on the oven,
Memorize the phonepad,

Learn to water the plants
by sound and volume,

Arrange everything in the cupboards
by size, shape.

Decide whom to trust,
how to store your language now.

Subconscious

       sweater frayed,
edges crumble on the floor,
          moth-eaten,
small pool of black lint
following

not poor,
      just sentimental

how she wore it, naked beneath,
when you came home the day after

years and lovers later
you still wear it at times, a secret,
for her smell, long gone, even on days
that you've forgotten her last name
      where she moved on to

Sestina for murder

Sssshhhhhhh. Don't scream. Not yet.
Wait until we're further out, so I can enjoy it.
Oh, don't worry. You'll get to know me soon.
I'm death. Well . . . yours, little girl. I am the death
that draws hunters to hunt you down, sweet-walkers of city streets,
your skin flashing like neon in the night.

I do all my best hunting at night.
One hundred millennia and they haven't found me yet.
While for me the hunting's easier — for you, and for him./
      Look in his eyes, you can see it;
I'm in here. He doesn't know what's got into him, but he will/
      . . . soon.
I'd say it's nothing personal, but nothing's/
      more personal than death;
more intimate. Have some pride: you've been chosen/
      from all the world's streets.

I was around long before there were streets,
but it's more fun this way. And simpler. Fires and caves/
      were the death of my night,
for a while. But I'm adaptable. Stop moving/
      or I'll tie you tighter yet.
No, there's no door handle on that side. You won't find it;
I only lost a few that way. And' I'm not about to lose you too soon.
This isn't TV, little girl. This is the real thing. This is death.

It's not true I'm picking you younger, you know. I've always/
      loved you as far as possible from natural death.
Look, we're almost there now. I only do the hunting on city streets.
The good stuff happens out here, where the only ones watching/
      are me and the night.
I suppose you're an obsession. But the novelty hasn't worn off yet.
It's what I do. You see, I lost something; I'll tear you apart/
      'til I find it.
Mind what I tell you. You won't have to listen long./
      It'll just be the knife soon.

The thing to remember is that you can't die too soon.

48

That's what I love about you girls, how much you think/
        you're fighting death.
I can see you thinking, like all the rest — all the things you wanted/
        from those pretty streets.
But it would have been a boring life anyway, little girl:/
        work-a-day, breeding, TV at night.
You weren't that bright, nothing special,/
        even if you couldn't see it yet.
Now I'll make you something special. Get out. Lie there./
        You're going to help me do it.

Every minute of every day I can find a man somewhere/
        thinking about it;
I just give him the courage. That's it. Scream now./
        No one will find you anytime soon.
I'll make you famous, though. For a few weeks./
        People love to hear about death.
Makes them feel they've accomplished something,/
        survived the dangers of the streets.
Women like to feel they've escaped me. The men feel . . . /
        That's it, little one. You've been a good girl tonight.
Wait — there's one more thing I want from you yet.

Well, it's been fun, little girl, but there are so many others yet,/
        waiting to help me find it.
The morning's headlines will be yours soon, though,/
        screaming callous murder, brutal death.
Don't worry about me, though. I'll be fine./
        The streets are always full, no end to the night.

Good Enough

Anne Le Dressay

Anne Le Dressay grew up in rural Manitoba, first on a farm near Virden, then on an acreage outside Lorette. She has been publishing sporadically since the 1970s, and has published one book, *Sleep Is a Country* (Ottawa ON: Harbinger / Carleton University Press, 1997), and two chapbooks, *This Body That I Live In* (Winnipeg MB: Turnstone Press, 1979) and *Woman Dreams* (Ottawa ON: above/ground press, 1998). She first moved to Ottawa to do her M.A. at Carleton, then her Ph.D. at the University of Ottawa. She taught for 10 years in Alberta, then returned to Ottawa in 1999. She is now a civil servant.

Heat wave

In the humid heat that has settled as if to stay,
the city is a mirage—forms distorted, colors blurred,
edges wavering. The heat shimmer is not a haze
in the distance, but so close that walking is like
pushing through water.

From just across the street, the old bank building looks
soft at the edges: pillars and cornices in grey stone
frame windows two stories high, set in red brick.
Its details are blurred, its colors dim. The heat
is more visible than the stone.

Two people have climbed to a shoulder-high ledge
out of the pedestrian traffic, out of the direct sun,
and they are posed there in the bottom corners
of the stone window-frame, as if they are
part of the design.

Each sits with back to a pillar of weathered stone.
They face each other, she with legs stretched out in front,
he with knees bent. There is not enough room
for both to stretch out fully. They are talking
intently, bodies languid in the summer heat,
all energy in their words.

They wear the uniform of the supermarket
whose new bulk incorporates the old bank building:
black pants, dark green caps and apron,
orange t-shirt.

Against the tired brick and stone, the orange
of their t-shirts is bright as a flag, the only thing
vivid enough to subdue the blur, the only anchor
in the floating world of mirage.

A small thing

A small thing happened on this dirt road
from nowhere to nowhere, a back road between
fields where no houses were.

A summer shower turned the dirt to mud and
clogged the wheels of a bicycle.
There was no traffic at all, no traffic in sight
except distantly on the highway.
Just the mud and the cyclist miles from home
with a bike she could not abandon
because it was not hers.

The wooden bridge within sight, the bridge with
no side rails, so narrow only one car could cross
at a time. Nothing happened. But what *could?*

> *The one car on a muddy road*
> *not a friendly neighbor. The one car*
> *driven by a bad guy who wants to get you*
> *under the bridge, and what do you do?*
> *Only the fields and no houses.*
> *Only the bush and the deep ditch and*
> *the long grass and the mud.*
> *Only the lonely spot on a lonely day*
> *and you can't get home.*

Nothing happened. The one car on the muddy road
was a friendly neighbor, a real one. He put the bike
in the trunk and drove her to the highway (the long way
home), then cleared the mud from the wheels before
leaving her to the rest of her adventure: a flat tire,
another summer shower, a friendly stranger driving her
to the gas station so she could call home, then her father
annoyed and refusing to drive out to pick her up 3 miles
from home with her brother's useless bike, so
she would have walked, pushing it all the way,
but her brother came.

Heirlooms

I have given away the silver brooch
that found its way to me in the dispersal
of my one grandmother's possessions after
she died. I have given away the gold ring
my other grandmother gave me when I was
13. I have given them to my oldest niece's
daughter. For years I kept the ring and the
brooch in a box, never wore them, looked
at them sometimes with puzzlement:
what could they be to me?

I have never wondered that about the prayer book
my father gave me when he was dying.
It had been his grandmother's. It is battered,
water-stained. I cannot read it. It is in two
languages that are not my two. I can recognize
some of its Latin words, phrases, whole
prayers: *Pater, Credo, Ave.*

Its other language is Breton, which descended
no further than my grandparents. From placement,
from parallels with the Latin, I recognize the word
for *God.* From similarity to Latin or French,
the words for *power, will, truth.* But I cannot
read it.

Sometimes I pick it up and leaf through it,
trying to make meaning of the words.
I think, *My great-grandmother read this,*
prayed with this. My father kept it, read
perhaps the Latin, made out perhaps
more of the Breton than I do. When he knew
he was dying, he chose me among his
children to have it.

It lives on a shelf among my other books.
When I pick it up and browse through it,
I am with my father, with his grandmother
praying

There is always dust

Every time I move, I believe
(in some dim and inarticulate recess
of my brain) that in this new home, *this* one,
finally, there will be no dust.

The light will always be pure.
Everything I own will find its proper place
and settle there, glowing, and will continue to glow.

And I will too. I will be my best self
every day. I will no longer procrastinate. I will
sit at my desk, and the sun will fall upon my shoulders,
upon my head, upon my words, and I will write
clean and perfect poems.

But there is always dust.

There is the dust of former tenants
lodged in corners, at the backs of shelves, in
light fixtures and in walls. There is the dust I bring with me
in my cardboard boxes, in my furniture, in my
books. There is the dust of the house itself, and there is
the inescapable dust of myself, into which I fall
daily.

I sit down to write, and the sun is not a single
golden beam, but a glare that picks out every
speck and mote upon the floor, the shelves,
and in the mocking air itself. There is no
stillness. Phantom brooms and mops invade
the flow of words, chase away metaphors.

And I am still myself. I sit restless at my desk,
distracted by anxieties, nagged by the small guilt
stirred up by the phantom brooms. I still
wrestle with rags and pieces of words
that will not form one perfect shining shape.
Nothing changes. I am still myself and
there is always dust.

Even the cockroaches

When I came looking for an apartment,
he didn't ask for references personal or financial.
He asked me where I worked. When I said,
The university, he was impressed. I could tell
he wanted to ask more, but he didn't.
I didn't tell him that my paid work took
12 hours a week, that my income was
nowhere near my expenses, or that my savings
were nearing oblivion. He rented me the apartment.
By then I knew he just couldn't say no.

He couldn't say no to anyone else either.
The smell of marijuana sweetened the halls.
The previous tenants in my apartment had left
in a hurry, the caretaker said. They were wanted
for possession of stolen goods. They had not left a
forwarding address or informed their business
associates. For months, strangers buzzed me
from downstairs or knocked on my door.

Turnover was high. The landlord said yes
to every applicant. The fugitive and the transient,
the slightly illegal and the eternally restless found
temporary shelter.

I was on the edge of dramas, in the margins of stories
more vividly colored, more luridly violent than my own.
I felt like an extra in a movie whose script
I had not read. I stayed on the sidelines, uneasy,
waiting for clues, an outsider by the quietness of my life.

I exchanged greetings politely with the reserved young
cop across the hall. The landlord could not say no
to the law any more than he could to the lawless.
Once or twice I looked after the caretaker's
small daughter when he had errands to run (his
wife in the hospital with complications from childbirth).
Next door to the cop, a very large man would leave
his door open and listen for me and come out in the hall

to stare at me as I fumbled my keys. He would ask
innocuous odd questions that startled me out of reserve
and then deeper in.

It was not a world whose rules I understood
or would ever feel easy with, one in which
outward lives mixed easily: favors asked and given,
beds briefly shared. Reserve was of a different kind
than in my world.

Even the cockroaches living their secret lives in the walls
were more at home than I was.

In my cool cool basement apartment

Spiders have had babies in my cool cool
basement apartment with its floor of golden
stone so cool and smooth underfoot
and its deep marble windowsills.

Spiders have been fruitful and their progeny
have no enemy but their own numbers.

High and low, webs and single threads
become dustily visible in every
angle and corner.

Everything that does not move
is connected to something else—
the clock to the headboard it sits on,
the toaster to the counter, the cat's dish
to the floor, one lamp to another.
Invisible threads slide sticky fingers
across my skin as I walk through my rooms.

Little spiders, barely visible, hang from
cupboard doors, from utensils I take from a
drawer, from the top rim of my glasses.
They scuttle for safety as I pick up the dishcloth,
or a book I was reading this morning.

I battle the invasion with broom and vacuum cleaner,
but the fine sticky threads reappear.
I begin to fear that one morning I will wake
like Gulliver, staked to the bed by multitudinous
silken cords while busy weavers bind me
tighter, closer, connecting me finally, visibly,
irrevocably to everything I own.

Good enough

He tells me that
if I join an internet chat group,
I can be whoever I want.

I can be a 21-year-old
super-model.

Perhaps he thinks this to be
the secret fantasy
of every middle-aged woman.

He is too young to drink or vote.
He lives on line, chatting
electronically
with people halfway around the world
or just across the room.
He lives several lives
at once.

To his mind, he is
opening my eyes to exciting
possibilities.

He doesn't know that,
even at 21, I didn't want to be 21.
I wanted to be older.

Or that what I crave is not
the limelight, but
anonymity.

Or that I have never wanted to be
a model of any kind or super
of any kind.

Good enough
is good enough for me.

Every Morning

Every morning a boy waters the sidewalk
in front of McDonalds. He uses a black hose
attached to the faucet in the red brick wall.
Sometimes he waters the red brick wall too,
washing dust from the graffiti so that
they stand out boldly, black scrawl on red
brick: a happy face, an obscenity, *Make the
rich pay*. He waters the dust, the concrete,
the absence of any green growing thing.

The slow hush of water competes with
traffic noise : small gurglings, tiny streams,
placid flat surfaces where the sidewalk
traps small lakes. He waters the whole sidewalk,
wall to curb, careless of the feet of passersby
who step gingerly through his small flood,
careless too of the black snake of the hose
uncoiling behind him, nipping at people's feet
with sudden loops.

The boy waters the sidewalk as if it were
a lawn or a garden. He waters the wall.
The graffiti flower. The concrete whispers
gratefully, like leaves in rain.

Anniversary

A year ago, I took a government French test
in the morning, and in the afternoon I took
my cat to her death.

Now I am fully bilingual as the government of Canada
judges bilingualism. Now the government will never doubt
my ability to serve the public in either official language
or even both at once.

Now I live in a cleaner, quieter, emptier apartment.
No cat hair, no litter dust, no vomit on floors or furniture.
No cat frenzies as she gallops from room to room. No
interruptions of my work by one who does not recognize
the relevance of books and paper. No interruptions of my sleep
by a head-butting hello. No

welcome at the door when I get home. No warm weight
curled against me on cold nights. No rumbling purr
on my pillow. No quiet calm presence stretched along the back
of the sofa as I read or watch TV.

I speak English. I speak French. I never did speak Cat.
Not really. Though there was communication, and, I hope,
some real understanding. It's hard to say.

I slip more and more easily from English to French and back.
I grow more accustomed to noises in the night that I cannot attribute
to a cat. The quiet in the apartment when I am home alone
no longer tastes so emphatically

of absence. Time passes.

On discipline

discipline—a whip used to inflict chastisement on the body as a means of mortification; used in religious (or other) self-flagellation
        New Catholic Encyclopedia (and other sources)

I'd been thinking I have lost my sense of discipline.
I have grown lax. I think about what I ought to do,
and I put off doing it until I feel like it,
and if I never feel like it, what ought to be done
is not done.

But I can call that up that kind of discipline
at need, though only with effort. It is the *other*
discipline I have lost—the whip that persuades
from thought to action.

It takes me months to talk myself out of the fantasy
of seducing an old friend, of confessing
a lust that has lain dormant for years and that I
persistently pushed under when we were part of
each other's lives weekly instead of annually.

It takes me several tries over as many years
to call back out of memory and conviction
the energy to put myself aside when I teach,
to focus on them instead of me. It takes me
that long to learn again to give myself away,
as I once did without thinking in almost
every class.

It is not discipline I have lost, but the *lash*
that overcomes inertia. I have mislaid
the knotted cords and the habit of submission
to their sting. I have lost

a sense of sin, a lively conscience to convince me
that mere intention is a failure of the soul,
of which God takes note. I have given up
the guilt that burned each lapse into the soul
like the welt raised by a well-wielded whip.

Belief lingers, but more distantly than in the days
of prayer and repentance, of constant re-
turning to the details of the world and the will
of its maker.

The knots of a remembered discipline,
lie lax. My palms recall the grip
of the handle; my back remembers the bite.
I remember those. But not

the desire to wield it.

From my Office Window

I thought she was kicking at the leaves
as she walks across the soccer field
leaning hard against the wind,
but she has a bouncy little brown thing
on a leash and seems to be kicking
some object for it to chase.
I can't see the object. It's too far and
I forgot my glasses again.
I can't even see for sure
if the bouncy brown thing is a dog,
though it must be. Cats don't come
in that shade of brown and don't
walk so willingly on leashes.
It could of course be some entirely
different bouncy animal, and *she*
might even be *he* in these days
of indiscriminately cultivated long hair.
It's just that I think I recognize
that blob of blue as a particular sweater
that goes with that color of yellow hair
on a particular person.
I should have remembered my glasses.
Then I could have spoken with certainty
about the dog and the nature of the
object kicked and whether the walker
is *she* or *he* and maybe even told you
who. She is gone now and the dog too,
or whatever it was, and the soccer field
is empty of detail, though if I had my glasses
it might not be.

Photograph

Karen Massey

Karen Massey's poetry has appeared in the online pdf Ottawa poetry journal *ottawater*, and in Canadian publications and anthologies including *Shadowy Technicians: New Ottawa Poets* (Fredericton NB: cauldron books / Broken Jaw Press, 2000), and the chapbook *Bullet* (Ottawa ON: above/ground press, 2000). She received an M.A. in English Literature (Creative Writing) from Concordia University and her work has won national and local prizes including the *Joker is Wild* and the *Jane Jordan Poetry Competition*.

Photograph

A woman on the prairie visiting her mother's
abandoned childhood home
A woman on the beautiful, bald prairie
with her ailing mother, returned to her homestead
left alone over time in a place called Holdfast
A woman at fifty absorbing some of the
spilt emotions her mother rarely shows;
her mother dancing nearly childlike beneath the huge-hued sky,
her body unusually spirited, resounding in rare laughter
A woman with a borrowed camera taking b&w photographs
of the deserted house and prevalent memories
A woman on the unforgettable prairie;
sad woman, beautiful women, on the prairie
An idea of dust and memory caught in gray scale,
the spell of years broken around them;
the mother uncharacteristically fey
and the daughter, gorgeous, slipping into that middle age
that has its own vision and endless sky
Two women, a shimmering, broken open
in Holdfast; the woman as open as the sky -
her mother, the sky, as close as they've ever been

Cold Water Wash

The midwives are gone, everything is still,
you're sleeping with our baby eight hours in this world
and I'm watching,
unwilling to sleep, to let the day slip past

Here in near-darkness,
snow piling up outside, I can't let this feeling cleanly end,
won't let the day leave without leaving
as deep a mark as it can

Here, in this apartment, a baby was born;
here in this small space, beneath a small statue of Odin
another mother and newborn finally touched skin
and now, hours later, who could tell,
except for a kitchen counter of emptied mugs and drinking glasses,
faint streak of blood on the hall closet door jamb,
you'd never know what transpired here today;
I pushed a baby out of my body

with so little supporting evidence; a camera
of assorted exposures, small bag
of garbage, a bag of bloody laundry
headed for cold water

Not even realizing
the ways I'll turn nostalgic for this afternoon,
wishing, for example,
to have the bloodstains return to the shirt I was wearing
this snowy Thursday afternoon in December when I first held you
and my life changed forever,
the slate wiped clean

Winter Afternoon Zen

Winter light purifies
it's the voice we ache to hear
lover we long to remember
drawing bright fingers across
the dark branches of winter trees–
No use,
every metaphor tosses out jumbled;
since your birth I can't look at any same world
Around us the world whirls   is whorls
whips past, days dissolve into daynightday

All light refracts through you
your centring just happens   *is*
You know only trust and fate
and being

I try to decypher you
swathe you in metaphors entirely foreign to your skin
Your breathing simply   *is*

The world pulses in your blue iris

August

Only so much abundance that you can take up before things go to seed, the hours flow into the trough of the calendar: spent. What happens with these breezes? Where do the hours go? Always, so much forced into each memory, I can drive round the bend of unfamiliar highway and run headlong into the memory of a forgotten auto trip, the family on cloth and vinyl upholstery, three sisters seat-belted into the back of the Biscayne, watching and listening at every curve.

Where were they headed, those girls with their pixie-cuts and innocence? Where are they now, those daughters with their sunhats and freckles and enviable rapport? Summer winds down, the torch-lit parties trail off later and later into the night before they venture back inside, the conversation slows but deepens, fans its context and implications out over the darkened room like heat. How did it get to be late August? Did you ever think we'd make it this far, all those years ago, hanging with friends at the drive-in, sitting in classrooms, figuring our ages in the year 2000? We honestly believed we'd be dead by now, burnt out on dope or culled by cancer or something tragic, but modern. And then the August a hush crushed us when a peer suicided. Until then we'd never guessed it was an option; until then it waited far off in the realm of *Other*. Afterward, every noun kept a shadow close. We'd never seen that world before, had never noticed; life like a late-summer garden, all growth invisible in the roots. Now, wherever we go, there it is, blooming and fading; that always unexpected little shimmering in the ordinary—

Not a Sonnet

Where are they now, young bodies on the streetcar
heading out for food after hours and hours
building and unbuilding one another's bodies,
glimpsing the soul's secret sorrow and passion.
Good night, here comes the snow,
there's no TV here, just a stereo and a cat or two
and a pile of blankets on what we've deemed a bed,
though we never sleep, we're so young and our bodies feel
as if we're running out of time and this timelessness
is all we've been made for. It's always night here,
stars work just for us, seasons pull in and out of months;
spring outside now, kids noisy in the school playground,
pushing bodies through the air— they don't even know yet
what they've been brought here to do

good!

Triggers

Saturday night in darkness I contemplated firearms,
how after every shift when Dad came home
he'd empty the six chambers, lock his handcuffs through the
mechanism, e ?
and secret the gun and bullets God knows where.
His .38 calibre service revolver. Something we only saw holstered,
and the time I'm describing. It seemed a different thing
from what he wore to work, loaded,
the possibility for death carried silently at his hip.

Last night a phone call
brought the news of your car accident,
the outcome unknown. Three thousand miles away
we're scattered family phoning siblings and hospital wards and
awaiting results;
you got air-lifted back to the Northern city you'd spent hours
driving away from.
Now it's late in the middle of my night and I'm thinking
too many things, it's three hours ahead here and I'm filling these hours,
cramming them with too many questions and memories and
shooting holes in them
with my wondering if we'll ever hold another conversation at our
same level,
wondering what happened, the hard details, the less than subtle impact,
possibility of head injury—

Is it bad? Would it shock you to wake up
and see me there in your time zone, the hours and answers lost,
your body
hooked up to monitors and intermittent sleep, the simple
unknowing of it,
how these things happen always over distance.
Today I stood dumbfounded in a store and sought greeting cards to send
to addresses I've memorized because somehow
most of those whose lives share meaning with mine live at a distance.
Nothing fancy, a smart hello, sent without mentioning,
but completely distilled from the impetus
of loss. Every day
we waken into mortality yet today I felt the giddy surge

that it's all true—
and none of us are ready.

How like these things to course up from out of the blue,
how like them to snap at us with their elastic resilience and
seductive allure.
I couldn't cry. I sat
staring into a night shot through with stars,
stared into nothing and waited and remembered
and waited. Suddenly that bruise on my hand from—what?—faded.
I saw only the inner pulsing, a shimmer like heat around light
sources and people.
I could see you in the hospital, IV from your hand like a queer
umbilicus,
so much clinical white backdrop and the tip-toeing ministering of nurses
in and out of the sleep you were pulling yourself through weakly,
pulling hand over hand like climbing a rope to the top of an incline,
all because of the promise of scenery. And that's where I left you,
staring out from that dizzy height, that whole visual world you've
always laid claim to—
that may or may not again show up in your paintings—and I waited,
thinking things I might never be able to ask you, triggering
questions you might never get to ask me.
Two nights before I'd been pondering the havoc that could come
from something as small as a bullet, fired from a gun.
In one split second. Today I see
how that's no different from the impact of news of a sister
sent over distance through the tidy space of a wire
on a Sunday night in the white-washed middle of April

and how pathetic I can become
hooked up to this telephone like it's state-of-the-art, a finer heart
monitor
than it really is,
like it's capable of sending the answer to questions,
say, the quotient of the equation posed by impact over distance
divided by time
and how that is always *love*, no matter the variables;
quietly locked up and stored in some secret, dark place. And why?

gypsy moth

things that fly, things that are engineered, are built
by human hands; things that are vintage now,
are part of our war history   versus

the poetic name of an insect, *Lymantria dispar*, the females of which
do not fly,
given to an aeroplane, because we humans *can*

think of gypsies, of concertinas and laughter, of raggle-taggle
vagabonds singing and footstomping around a fire, sparks
randomly spiralling skyward   starlight and fluid women twirling,
clad in movement

and the moth: ugly, ravaging caterpillar, beautified by a vagabond
name

and the aeroplane, and the men who fought and flew her

O beautiful name, *gypsy moth*,
that dissolves on the tongue like a powder, like a hollow burnt taste

like the moth herself,
witnessing her brother
dancing too close to flame   pauvres petites,
poor Daedelus' daughter

Prayer

Talk spills out of you the way light peeks past a door cracked open, easing pure white into the saffron-scented kitchen at 3 am. You never rest. Demons crawl in and out of your thoughts in a way that lets you feel them marking their movements like pieces plotted on a chess board, dragging whole and broken bodies across your brain. O voices the rest of us can't reckon with: O voices you hear with their strange and sad tales, their other-world urgings. Jump, they whisper, half test, half incantation. You reach into their conjurings and make the jump: the spiral of time against the spiral of your body cradled in despair and youth and your fey beauty and prickling genius and in the few seconds it takes, your body splinters like an icicle fallen to the sidewalk. Strangers rescue you and doctors mend you with surgery and morphine and your family wraps resolve and worship tighter. You are purified: a sound going into the vacuum, the one love that saints and sages and idiots all feel. We marvel at the way you beat mortality and show how you can win. We marvel at your flip disregard for the body—we who are older and have given birth know nothing of that sheer vitality and fear death more readily each day. Your sheer happiness and sadness is archetypal; it calms and scares me. You bring that other world here in one cracked breath and smile, in any grimace cracked against your flawless cheeks. I wish for you a grounded power to root you in a tolerable pose. While they race time to fuse your broken vertebrae, I hope your truth leaks out onto their scalpels.

Giving Birth

You want me to say how it was agony,
how the full moon slipped through her moorings, escaped,
rounded by fluid and a separate heartbeat, the world, my
new mission, this unspeakableness–
you want me to admit how the pain seared, how
it was primal and archetypal, the most useful
thing I'd ever done   And it was

You want me to admit I was brave,
or crazy, to be drugless and at home;
you want me to say that I screamed blue murder
and called to the saints individually and frequently
but I was quiet   The day wedged through me with its
winter storm, white light and restless night, contractions
spaced through those silent hours
and none of the other tenants even suspected

I was too quiet,
trudging the tundra far off in my head
on a squall-racked day at the end of the century
Thursday   Ottawa snow storm:
these are the facts—
and on hallway linoleum between two bedrooms,
beneath small casts of Odin and the patron saint of writers,
I pushed a small, perfect body out of my own

You want me to say I was frightened and alarmed,
but I was ecstatic and alive
on a wild, wild high that crested for days
It seemed strangely akin to doing mushrooms—
but indescribably more intense and otherworldly
And less psychedelic And without the sex

Near Dawn

Songbirds make small talk beneath the sky-squawk of seagulls,
even the nearby room with sixteen young men
and a bathtub of bottled beer
is quiet
and a baby sleeps
beneath the faint hiss of rain Our baby

We conjured him in a North Bay motel
and here we are in Windsor,
while the world spins on its same axis,
travelers still awaken early,
dry hands on another anonymous white towel
then unbolt the door to another day

But now we have this future to remind us who we used to be
and I've become a woman with a backpack of toys and nonsense verse,
love-blind and humble,
surrendered to the spell we cast that March

We pack in darkness
while in the bed, the small breathing of a sleeping boy,
arms outstretched, the face of his father tucked into his skin
Our baby sleeps,
belly full of breast milk,
life filling with possibility

I want to watch you now,
draw the moment around us particle by particle,
fit you into memory with the same indelible ink
as the story of your birth
I don't want to borrow your privacy
to wrap inside these sheets:
your whole life is wide open space
I feel guilty, even now,
betraying your perfect sleep with description

I release you from the page as we go into the day,
picking you up in a waking bundle
that stirs into alertness surprisingly fast

76

Bloodlines

for M Pook, in England

This is the light that makes one hopeful,
walking in frigid, crystalline air,
breath held briefly, eyes high,
cut open by wind-chill

But spring is coming!
We all say it and mean it,
while winter with its stalled cars and weak batteries
turns over again and again
The power keeps coming on with the flick of a switch,
the ice storm is etched onto memory
like filigree on glass

and along the highway, broken treetops surrender
and archways of doomed white birches wait to thaw—

continue with seasonal plans to send leaves sunward into

the possible—

*

As if everything were this easy
the blood ticking rhythmically through arteries
red message in the heart cells
carbohydrate speaking in mitochondria:
an order for each system, imposed by nature

to pick up a pen, or better, an instrument crafted from surgical steel
and begin to slowly navigate
what it is in us

in order to illuminate what can go awry:
pulsing nebulae of darkness
absolute cold in the body
minute face of death
staring from the inert microscope field

or smaller:
magnification via speeding electrons
captured on film
It is through love you unwind this labyrinth
strand by strand   O Muse   O double helix

It is truth you seek to disclose
where it has masqued itself
as a little black lie
bent over and gasping
shameful

Siren wailing soundlessly
mutation   mutayshun

*

As if anything else were easy:
in a few keystrokes   your words are here
or, simply
I key you in   my ordered consonants & vowels   message
to press [Enter]
and send communication electronically
via coded cables crossing under the ocean

electrons beamed nearly instantaneously
to and from you whom I hold kindred
and have never met

filling our days with data
charting ever smaller portions
we seekers of cures

while all around us cells bloom and fade
like fruit trees ruffled in blossoms
springtime sentences fragrant with life
and promise

*

if only to mention
casually, the body in all of its circuitry
the workings and misgivings of DNA
Your life of passion: molecular genetics,
attentions focusing the twisted spiral
we carbon-based can only praise and lay to blame

height and body: DNA
love of music, poetry: DNA
fear of injury:
migraine:
love:

I try to reduce the simplest of events
to something simpler   stilled
I do it in awe
in deference to you who can look into
bases distilled from genes unraveled from tattered pairs of chromosomes
and explain countless miracles   re/generations

I ascribe to writing things carefully
the intent behind these cells
hell-bent for reproduction
I argue spring blossoms over these snow drifts
and heavy snow clutched by dark branches
versus you   /untangling the invisible

O you and your ability to see through time
to unlock simultaneous future and history
unravel its broad ribbon of meaning

To you who can see through cells and touch their impetus:
I raise my vial of RH+ ink
along with this warm sunshine:
all I am

La Mémoire du Corps

Una McDonnell

Una McDonnell has performed her work at readings and music festivals, on top of café tables, and on one occasion in a boxing ring. She attended the 2002 Banff Wired Writing Studio and the 2003 Sage Hill Poetry Colloquium. She has published work in *Arc*, *Prairie Fire*, and the anthologies *Written in the Skin: a poetic response to aids* (Toronto ON: Insomniac Press, 1998) and *Musings: An Anthology of Greek-Canadian Literature* (Montreal QC: Vehicule Press, 2005).

Desperate Swimmers

(After a mixed media work by Betty Goodwin, *Untitled*, 1994-1995,
graphite and oil stick over gelatin silver print on translucent mylar
film, 94 by 71 cm).

This lone figure floats, face-down
in a subcutaneous sea—
he could be making love, or dead

on a bed of nerves. See how he is sinking
when his body longs to be taut?
Taught. Everything we need to know

is held in the body. The skin, a windworn gate-
keeper barring the world from celled
inmates who record our days in their own

arcane language. Our bloody emergence
in the world, penned there, the body
we leave, imprinted. If I could translate

one woman, one man. I write them
in love, if only for an hour.
I am coupled to a drawn man, his death

dance, untold stare in skin and what lies
beneath. I want to open
him, spread him against this graft,

love him nerve-bouncing raw. Doesn't he
know? Don't I? We sink
into our own bodies. He has traded breath

for wisdom: how long can he suppress
breath? How deep is deep enough
in the language of skin? Hours

between two people click past
as cells divide. I will never touch
the hand that touched me first. Never
—like this desperate swimmer:
drowning, dead, or dying
for answers—stop staring into skin.

Grieving Knife

(After a mixed media work by Betty Goodwin, *Grieving Knife*, 1991,
pastel and graphite on translucent mylar film, knife, 85.5 by 71 cm).

If there is an edge to this, I want to run
my palm along its steel sharpness, let blood
pool and gather until I can float—
an embryo with no cord but my own

small yearning. Somewhere there is an
ancient song. Its rhythms live in skin.
Its slow strum, a choke-throated Ah—
knotted in my tongue, warming words

in my mouth but never speaking.
Will I ever sing me? I have been
given away. Grief follows
the lost child with a stalkers' grace.

His knife at my throat, exacting
its price: one family
for another. I take the blade
and in its glint, see my own

fractured reflection. Feel its cold metal
weight in my hand. When I have it,
I use it. With a wretched precision
I tell my first self: You are not real,

of earth, or born. Here, I say.
Cut here. I am
blessedly exact. Conclusions
are satisfying, but bloody.

Villanelle: Birthmother

Your love against time. And distance did not alter
how he bent you in dark water with such force.
Your hand on the door does not falter
the day you tell him. Fury has made you a martyr.

A vein cannot with wishing change its course;
your love against time and distance did not alter
his soul. But in your battered belly ardour
grows for this life snaked within you: life-force.

Your hand on the door does not falter:
Her good life will leave you no regrets, consider
time a healer: the sweet, smart social worker's discourse.

Your love, against time. And distance did not alter
the place where her curling body marked your centre.

Now she stands on your step; you breathe a measured space.
Your hand on the door does not falter.

Doors that close, lock down, open later —

Though you tremble, step forward, into nature's course,

your love — against time and distance *did not alter*.
Your hand on the door does not falter.

Agape

For you I will become the stoneless olive, pulled warm
from leaves, slyly entered and perfectly left: intact

but barren inside the circle. In the dream of a child, the man
looks at the girl with unflinching interest. She will mistake

this for that pull she feels as he winks and strides, lone,
in his own direction. On the road, the roll of tires

hitting gravel and the singe-sound of crickets. She opens
the door, *Efharisto*, steps inside. She is willing to risk the dark

locus of a strange, estranged man—his blood and its pressure
in her veins. *E agape mou yia sena,* she might say, *my love for you,*

the gape of it inside me. Tonight, she will sleep inside the moon
of her small silver tent. Pour careful water over hot coal,

watch smoke as it rises, slow, into night—

Sore Eros

The mind
is a mapped

labyrinth.

Experience marks
its trial along brain tissue.

Without you—
        nothing
happens. The *you* that acts
marks

the trail; the trail
acts
on you.

Soft tissue: womb-whorl, a world.

Mark the sacred
space   moving   central:
inside,
accumulated
junk of experience.

At the centre
Circle
which way,
        do you turn?

Neglected child expects regret—
Grows up: one callous
Lover and
Another
Another.

Trick to the labyrinth:

The way in is the way out.

VII. Packing

(An excerpt from a series, entitled "Fierce Light." Based on a poem
by Diana Brebner, "Christmas Fire," from *The Golden Lotus*,
Netherlandic Press, 1993. The italicized lines are direct quotes from
"Christmas Fire," they appear here in the same order as in that
poem.)

In Memory of Diana Brebner (1956-2001) and Anya Brebner (1985-2001)

We are meticulous. Boxes are numbered
and lists made: 1) green clay fish-dish,

2) iron and copper candleholders (with candles),
3) Blue Willow china (handed down). Everything goes

into a box—after all, who can decide
what deserves to be kept? We find words

not meant for us: lines for a poem, and once, a list
you called, "Things That Are Good." It seems too small,

packing, listing: 1) my books, 2) my girls, 3) I am not yet
dead. In clean white cloth, I wrap a Wedgwood jug

once filled with gladiolus. The last box consumes
all that remains. Back brace, nurse's log, Dilaudid

in various doses, stuffed in the ragged mouth.
How we feed it, all the things we would keep

forever. *How we feed it, all the things we*
would have disappear. Our departed—lucent, white

tea cups: contain us, rapt, in a taped-box heart.

V. Opening, Years Later

(An excerpt from a series, entitled "Fierce Light." Based on a poem
by Diana Brebner, "Christmas Fire," from *The Golden Lotus*,
Netherlandic Press, 1993. The italicized lines are direct quotes from
"Christmas Fire," they appear here in the same order as in that
poem.)

In Memory of Diana Brebner (1956-2001) and Anya Brebner (1985-2001)

You come across it hiding
Christmas gifts or sorting, finally,

through the untouched room. Open it,
release the scent from her last breath, song

of delirious half-sleep. Lift out the silver
chain she wore, it pools into the palm

with all its delicate weight. *And, after Christmas,*
the tinsel and paper, the packaging we

disdain, all the barriers that keep our
mysteries under wraps, everything goes

to the fire barrel. Now we suppose we are done
with opening or the tight ball we make of our aging

grief, the concealing layers of activity, belief.
What remains in ash cannot be denied. The smoke

in our skin: Consider it a gift. Everything goes
in flame or years—we open ourselves

to the hurt, burnt world, take it rawly in.

III. The Importance of Placement

(An excerpt from a series, entitled "Fierce Light." Based on a poem
by Diana Brebner, "Christmas Fire," from *The Golden Lotus*,
Netherlandic Press, 1993. The italicized lines are direct quotes from
"Christmas Fire," they appear here in the same order as in that
poem.)

In Memory of Diana Brebner (1956-2001) and Anya Brebner (1985-2001)

When your cells went crazy, your room was perfect:
flowers and cards lined up like sparrows

on a rail. Writing feels like the balance between precision
and chaos. One line is feathered from the mind.

The other is thrown, or set upon. Felt.
Some things emerge from a dark place

beyond thought. It's not always possible
to say: this is the right place for this person, word.

Faith is required. It's too easy to lose your nerve.
A poem is as fragile as an unrequited lover or the body

of a hurt bird struggling to fly. As hard
as picking up the fallen bird, half-alive, fluttering warm

against the palm. Who can say if placement, timing is enough
to save a poem? A life. A different line-break

or another minute on the veranda. I don't know
how losing these bodies breaks us, but I live

in their flight—that brilliant moment between earth and sky.

The Heart's Dumb Memoir

Sepia and crimson are the colours
of the body: under oxygen, light,
under closed eyes. The film of life

passes, fades in the dim
eye of memory. Do not feed me

bloodless talk. I feel
your Adam's apple fist
in your throat. Love runs

its roulette circle and we stand
waiting, each, for our numbers:

The silver ball dances, hovers

on the line:
I want *your* number, you
want *hers* and she wants *mine*;

blood filters back
through the needle, then belts
into the body; the neon hiss

of a moth seeking light. Send me out
if you must, but skin me first, send me raw—

If not your glistening body—the steam, after

90

His voice and the dark throat

it rises from: scent of damp falling
leaves at 4 a.m., raw
face of the moon and the wind's rising
into rustle, crunch of red
veined leaves divining the rough
edge of winter, ghost-trees shifting

into black-blue light,
a river under ice and
the undulating band
of divelight, deep
in the deep, and deeper

in the season, frost
on the tongue, ice-licked, melting
snow caught in the throat,
sounding in the larynx
of a black sky,
crystallized breath
of stars, osseous

silver limbs
frozen in the act
of opening—

Looking Down Water

I.

I will tuck my eye into the smallest valve of my heart, bury it
at the root of a tall oak—then, then

you will not enter me. Skin, your voice, my ear, your breath
in the room as I breathe. At the base of the hard root

I am meant to change everything. Love differently. The heart
is a cruel knot. I wish it would slip itself
                                        undone. My finger on your forearm

did trace a screaming track, your chesthair rose like smoke
to the lean bones below your throat, the rattled air,
                                the moment,   a stone I held,
                                and somehow dropped...

Come winter. The river will freeze and when spring ice
breaks, bodies rise. The heaviest things stay down, silted—

II.

Who doesn't contemplate the river? The cool amber flow and down
silt clouds slow as we touch; the fish circles the worm. The patience

of grief, I can see the fist coming a long slow line in time into
the hit, a good crack, and think, huh—numb; then blood, bruise,

break. What gets called healing: Pain. The heart circles back
on itself. Inside its walls, sparse sweat-heavy rooms, dank

and prone to flooding. I cannot let go: Grief, hit
me, my earth-bound heart—it beats again again again...

years rip out like the fish-lured line, chasing the silver flash.
At the end of the reel, there I am, looking down water—

from solids, or, *strike-out* ~~(a suite)~~

rob mclennan

rob mclennan currently lives in Ottawa (since 1989), even though
he was born there once (1970). The author of a dozen poetry
collections, most recently *name   , an errant* (Exeter England:
Stride, 2006) and *aubade* (Fredericton NB: Broken Jaw Press,
2006), he has two more forthcoming — *The Ottawa City Project*
(Ottawa ON: Chaudiere Books, 2007) and *a compact of words*
(Ireland: Salmon, 2007) — as well as a collection of essays,
subverting the lyric: essays (Toronto ON: ECW Press, 2007) and
Ottawa: The Unknown City (Vancouver BC: Arsenal Pulp Press,
2007). As editor, he is putting the finishing touches on collections
of essays on the works of Andrew Suknaski, John Newlove and
George Bowering (Toronto ON: Guernica Editions,
forthcoming), as well as *There Is No Mountain: new & selected poems
by Andrew Suknaski* (Chaudiere Books, 2007). Editor/publisher of
above/ground press and *STANZAS* magazine (both founded in
1993), he also runs span-o (the small press action network -
ottawa), and organizes The Factory Reading Series at the Ottawa
Art Gallery, as well as the ottawa small press book fair (twice a year
since 1994). He regularly posts essays, reviews and other writing
at *www.robmclennan.blogspot.com*.

montreal

I would through me, then, begin

I keep dreaming of living alone

three apples & the bay city rollers

I need the distractions to carry me alert

the four horsemen of ottawa cabdrivers

~~the women of all cities break my heart~~

at the end of practice I begin

autobiography

the child of some & the father of one

a blue squall intercepts me; scream

the whole of the mountain invasive & changing

a sunlight lothario; as a dream ~~catches~~ intercepts sleep

when all numbers past & to come; two ~~coats~~ for flinching

in my sleep, I; bake beauty flesh out of bone

train

the form of the enjambment is open

through fourteen sleet, a wave of nausea clouds

I sit well above the station

corollary colours; rain on the window

tracks

~~she talked abt the boudoir in advance~~

the puddle on the sidewalk meets the fact

I want the mud to know how to settle

I am the silence that disturbs the ear

the traces of the art subsides

solids

the water in the cup bends w/ me

the fence at the back of the farm is an illusion
between trees

two fingers of rain is an accumulation
the day measures

my father in his notebook reminds me

~~my father~~ in the last place I was looking

house

in the mud in the field it grows

a two car garage w/ no landscaping

every poem talks to its own architecture

tokyo

I berate the form as unreliable

a line & string; releasing slip-knots scattered

if love can be qualified; a practical solution

~~cockburn sang, I never can sleep in yr arms~~

would that I could memorize the earth

I have left this fraction ~~of ontario~~ behind

striations

I have been diffuse all day

the frog in the blender is the joke that refuses ~~to die~~

the seat by the window is luckiest

I am in danger of shortly

if I told you, would your wedding ring

am I going on amount

tinker

the colour of the sample does not need to match
the open paint

when he started to write, saul bellows
removed the letter s

all the pink houses ~~in st lazare tingle~~

in the heavy rain; I had to leave my bicycle
by the bookstore

what does the water know

the last place I ever

abated

as she wrote, sonar ping on the porcelain

the weight of the paper mill stench is sometimes
too much to bear

between exposition & the act of the hand,
the beer behaves badly

when are you thinking of disappearing?

each to their own, the anatomy of settings; you cant
rush the perfect

from international bridge

reading wallace stevens

the bright mess of colour in the florists where brockwell
buys flowers for his wife

the deep coral hue of montreal
cannot be sold or bartered

the list of other people is ~~very long~~

triggers

she breaks my heart by name

where one thing further into & immediate

I dont remember anything abt the shore

will anyone remember that phones had bells

when you begin where do you begin

I am noting the submission of small mercies

my love changes & I would not have it fixed

rereading robert creeley

the woman in the diner is too long

the coffee less bitter with a cinnamon touch
in the filter

~~I suffer these breaks~~

I can only suggest so little

~~I can only suggest so much~~

comfort class

in the future would be called economy

love is a dog on a small brown hill

there is nothing I could breathe right now to tell

something

sometimes there is nothing else to do but fall
~~& wait to see how you land~~

she points her finger to the dog outside, & the van
w/ the unusual colour

have you seen one of those before

I am looking at the quick of medieval entry

I am ~~a project of dirt lost roads slowly~~ waiting

solar eclipse / ~~lunar eclipse~~

the sun is stronger ~~than the moon~~

I am learning the radicals ~~of carpentry & food~~

I am beginning to see the complexities ~~of love & the ease of re-entry~~

ones enthusiasm is infections; ~~hindsight 50-50~~

I am beginning to understand ~~some~~

at this speed, the train ~~punches holes in the air~~

adjunct

I know nothing of eden but the ~~lack of~~ parties would have probably killed me

I am looking back on eating an apple

the conductor is clear as the sky

the texture squeaks of the curds on my coloured teeth

everything credits to a lack of understatement

poem ~~(three dog night)~~

I stand a urinals chance away

we fall in & out of step

the dog at the end of the street barks at nothing

who am I to suggest

the house ~~is much bigger than~~ the shed

a corollary

the squeak of the cart is like a mouse

the tension that pulls us apart ~~& holds~~

I am studying the window the horizon

a buddhist phrase of corn is not profound

I am destination more than I am willing

I am left w/ song & water ~~paving~~
~~the same ground; covered~~

fire

proofing it right

the sequence of events is critical

if no the fire or the smoke or the trees

the speculation of time is question

these clouds thumbtack the hard moon

I am standing in the barn at seven

~~everything is not all right~~

the city

thinking squarely in the face

I ~~passion~~ trees; I ~~heart~~ the moon

exposition is not clear reason

the silo at the edge of barn as
old as I & crumbles

the city remembers bees

beauty squarely in the eye

could never ~~look me in the you~~

house

at some point it was a good ~~idea~~ to put the couch out

the house in glen robertson the hill stands

tim hortons coffee fresh as the ice

he says, when in rome. . .

instinct my critical song; ~~my failed life as a montreal go-go dancer~~

thighs out to ready; heart the wind

I am as proceedural as stone berth

harkening the telltale thump of heart all roads lead to

no more oldies; stop playing that *middle of the road shit*

I am dead outside

religion

the merit of association is punctuated

I heart & the world hearts me

brockwell laughs at ~~aphids, not~~ aphorisms

I am the other way around

the tree at the top of the hill ~~is~~ a red line

a suggestion of birds overwhelm

the water is think & reliable

if being afraid of the arc needs a bite-light

how trudeau used words

I am not abt to confuse presidents with prime ministers

dont you know ~~w~~here I am

resorting to the resort hotel ~~I am~~

half of the time the only living boy in the national capital ~~region~~

to strike is to be undone

the 60s; I missed our camelot by three

the door opens dust ~~a run; a pirouette~~

american fiction

most ~~original~~ circumspect & searching

where the ~~incident~~ instance of history
~~might occur~~

the old moves have been appearing in
disguised forms

a member or affiliated orthodox

I am poetry as poetry

I am writing this so ~~rob mclennan~~ can understand

ontario

a lode of bloodstone load

I sing long about california; a shakespeare of light

the fridge magnet will endure

I am; we just sound ~~good~~ enough

bottom on the act of words

I am singular~~ly nature; natural~~

the divine orders from here are always

a lake a line a lode; a stone

the thin line the radio brings fresh water

the middle years

to stop for a while & let life take care

the differences are between us on the cape

the slow will have of ~~sky; the~~ slow ~~will have of wind erosion~~

a skilled hand will still love you outdoors

I am looking out the best available

note that the notebooks ~~for catallus stop~~

I am brethren to ~~the~~ breath ~~line~~

critics & deniers have said

109

modern gothic speech

a line of difficulty track reported birds

a concision as demotic

I am a club a temple stone

in the sun am human literally

sinking the metonymic ties that bind marriage

she would love that tool of tongue

an adaptation of ~~maximum lost~~ human assets

is remarkable to conjure

bicycle music

I dont like things whose inevitability works against me

the hour is too discursively clear to be representative

I have nothing left ~~with which~~ to locate the ~~precise~~ moment

the lock; the resonance; the strongest sense

where is speaking under; spring

the fucker that stole my bicycle

a walk a step can bear its full rhetorical weight

from : an eye line : poems

Max Middle

Max Middle is engaged in several projects which have as their fulcrum a practice of poetry or making up. Disciplined in verse, he also works in sound and visual poetries. Under the Griddle Grin imprint, he edits and publishes the Puddle leaflet poetry series. As a founding member of the experiment known as the Max Middle Sound Project, he has been conducting investigations into performance poetry, art, noise and music with some very talented collaborators. The ensemble staged its debut performances during the 2004 Ottawa Fringe Festival. Middle is the author of three poetry chapbooks, *A Creation Song* (Ottawa: above/ground press, 2004), *smthg* (Ottawa: above/ground press, 2005) and *flow march n powder blossom s* (Ottawa: above/ground press, 2006) and was included in the anthology *Shift & Switch: New Canadian Poetry* (Toronto: The Mercury Press, 2005). An interview with Middle appeared in the first issue of *ottawater*, and more information, including audio files, can be found at www.maxmiddle.com.

an i or an I

if you put a solitary i or I
an i or an I on the page
it would hurt you
I know

dear jc

dear jc,
for so many fish
thank you
for bringing them
we liked the lobsters, the shark
the cool skin
and the octopus
you brought to our school.

A Menu

split
vinaigrette
baby
trout
blanc
braised
slow
zucchini
monsieur
warm
homemade
sun dried
goat
greens

b being still

beauty can be found
b being still
stood outside the gate
ages did was too shandy
meant much from the high place
wants mountain makes tea
mould can be lurching
ice ovr a little told
tells skimming in a float plane
slicks picked unsanguineous
safe to raise that arm again
the one with the pen in it
a tattooist decrees left to right
countermand stuff of crime
graphemes extracted simmering
man while manshie d d flew

faced me the reflection floats
in here this side of mirror
said i heard stood what was stolen
poondle basha full trash na go
alright i said fistula
genria janria chip kelta
stiff off the surface stick
stooshing mouth off walk
smooth schnorkel pipe smoker
strokes the shimmering water
a face stoking through the gate
pillows a sail on a rise futuring

C

cuz how el divo
spots of writing on a black dog

she never talks to me
speaker off key

left yellow on the stovetop
youth continues if you count

my sister spells my nightly
home to reassert it to be certain

an MMSP C poem

the MMSP soundsters C
munchie pff dhaA C c
rye hymes what u wish U C
in a bag a gag C
all along aClang
C we laugh

is never the never R u there

is the never the never R u there
zTrees not Uood lostiz
there zefrs woods lost like
chins scarred from centralizing cap's
clots termed for zentrillmmimming sLs
shalas honed home toothspliceZ
zallas blamd Dooming ooths less teeths
zad it was blamed for looming blums
episodic Baltic barking as feared
rotted into verse limes catch up to length
& whisper their end
frank as a carnival drummer
ears of dragons wave white branches of despair
pop up & run into width

centrifuged & gone to Crotan
then the next generation found
waz kept at the bay, water in there hidden
i wide hid if formed of the name postage
N the sedges cutz the ones U forgot
zero footages terms scrapped

the marbles in the flesh wards
mouthed bound hid like description

warbler adrift adrift
its driven in
the west wind
breast beaten

night planes cross
ghost passages

the gaunt man shrugs
caresses a supple clap

dream *S*

same dream *S* dreamt as

S dreamt rare *S* air.

zedders

zudders
z zS xxxxS
Smuk X
ZRUDmrs X
Z S
S Z
  s
  z

      s Z
      Z s

Zedsters Z and s less leadz tha ammo

A Zster SSer

SSer Zedder A

Petty Crime

the cops had dand
vand. alay dest iction
  req   vand   d esticion
     e sth   letic ians ath a lee
smitten hulk hunt up   spur
   trick   snake away
pat   trician
snatching titian

ate the rig

(or swing low the pang there)

which h ing U sym ment wish
uddrifudd d d u fi r d d u

sn nost tt red noz
stril nostr
nore sno ero ons ik
kit of snow of ing
short ee z for Y for zed s
your old ess gus hisses
snorts once
part 2 toe tap manic
cinch cashing machines

toadies wince once

which since
wins at their crickets
optimigraze me
by lead by i grade
watching wimp bands
slip as symmentry

sheep in / sheep at
harmony gravy a cat
clash a chord
clatter a can
slash slash slash
can can

in closh in
cash out cash
cupboards bare
hands type morph back
ed mop tuned
child mited

clean you will at the
limpling you won at the
ping lo le pang la
(swing low for a pang)
pinch

Some Jewelry

nothing off but for some jewelry
how it always was

then it was time to go
with someone caught up in frames

someone else had their glasses on backwards
to make a fuss inwards a question

the cook's mother never cared for me
despite the relish I took in eating

sat at the back with a guy cloaked in cobwebs
he spread rumours about himself

told the others where to hang up
they fret and flex about a hill upholstered

they talked about capping it with a flag
we spoke about putting it off

but someone has to tell them about the flock
oriented around wellness you can see fibre

lace

one page over ."& you knew it"
cover of low flying airplanes
a fire in Ottawa, winter
reaches ripple & calm

wanted bus laces, found an H
up a lean tall tree, a flush
wet birds flocking 'achoo!' past
a motor hums lost below ice

run scrummee

j U swh s y b Y

jj U so see holey

j uscrew seem only

U uscr seem Oh Y Y

U R su scu e em me

R U sum scuem meanie

run scrummee   tell   tell

a gleaner

a year since a gleaner chittered stubble
its chipmunk face down stirrer of glitter
remains once the day dug thru left nothing
but black & white fall of summer
& a billowing up of in grammar
on built over uneven ground
leaden swagger norths a burst river
a squirrel descends burrowed snares
braced a shrunken desert, hulks trill & rattle
felling gilded stars in hammerstroke
on the gleaning trail off another year
where your bloody stagger ends leafy
flying worm, you flummox the optic nerve
the season seeds nests from underground
today the floor remains to be swept
& a chipmunk scavenges without a predator
the circulatory system overflowing
pleasure rigs fruit to exit waves
the Buddha's absence responds face up
oxen adorn the raked trails of his passage
a mundivagrant seen wheeling the shadows
capturing silence & a draught of smoke
Buddha burgeoning the windward of/
fully

The New Wolves

It's been a month since
the wolves descended from airplanes
on bubbles and blew out the moon;
casting tracks filled by glass soldiers,
lit up, on blocks:
sentinels, silent at dusk.
The children are on the lake
to rouse kites to stillness
and the sound is slowly familiar
from a collapsed anteroom.
When they ride saddle less
with the full moon at dawn,
the spiders will awaken
as puppets strung in new suits
attending a ventriloquist's voice.

a kickstand down in five tercets

yup put kickstand down
offered an invitation but
& i'm stuck standing

you put kickstand down
offered an invitation fluff
still & i'm stuck standing

quick sand down & swim
sore elses mint the day
some knowledge 'n' chaff

kickstand 'n da sugar
in the shooting stars
stooped taxed red

now put down pipe yup
drain for work merely late
lit hype drooling the wing

For the Voice from the Breath (2)

chubberlery ye ant et atta reo tant yo eelittle russet reuse residue
srescue rug rue esey
run sur rash rat ran ras raz rak rallatara arb ara arer air able arble ab
A A b b b barable blub blab aa na a ash na na blush tink grusking
ging ging tringgin jot gin gan gong
chabalara roth stoff ran rosh ta takating ging ring gtring gung got jot
jam jong chunt unt
runting ran rant stoofer rosher tak ating ginger gunger gring gtring
sting gur T G ujje ho gee
ring gee strip string strafing stuck luck is not no take tuck as for
rakking RG knows why gee
antiseptic trip up ascetic smelling frog rog regress stoker stooked
mooged moon and money
paste gang peptic dissing dabbler delivered male peptiding gangs
pack up dissed babbling delivered mute
disable dishevel the cable diptheria docks stretch him trim twinng
and tug a lux chill
frug frug furred sharp station pain drill rate regress hollow hamp
rout rills
five fingers stung tigers stun yo yo reeeen go europo raka roroko
opho stowed ophiles frell riders pump
rent shine goes curb side runners gon rig flows curb side run pigged
yellow
wilt bam O shirting a cub a cube b flemish shout flow rubbed ruby
digged cello
hilts of skort wham O shorting a lisp a link B frumberish flout
yellow short flubbers beaconing
milk layer of filmers lewd and offensive raked off the screen
fumblish short and flixering asna pod
flickering in the moon sun yellow odor rag off offense scrammed
blubbling fumb bumble
clicked boons squelched borrow odells toothbrush for a final run
flummoxing flock tock betonk
ink way motors quell yard goes yellow with dandelion brush
runners flocking amongst clocks
burning pavement tires wellng dark aflo liate leer anta blant ishing
bork broked hosehandle
abiliating lee shame say we barking rark affination at lanting late the
rocked horse boke boke

129

shone honed leek stark away she she stared altinating atlan sharers
space pocked mark mortin
no not shingling her stare out shanks of bork ralteratting anklan
space sharing spock made mork
appler kind trog erger mashing parts to mook rorts oonkoonted ink
latter shored smock
drop gone
fog call trope of punish saver kanteen sheeld carrier kanched along
gongussing
brag lunch snag craggled above furstinlane cobbled shane stewed
tick too
sik clues too fuch oog od god sued the first in line tickled the last
ticks too
barking got them nowhere woofed the laxatives in line the barking
ticks shielded the towers
gagged alang clanging shooie
put bibs to prison ribs layings skins foffing locks gog agog in fog
toffed popped shaped furry moot on the logging fruit a biscus
translating fricless hibiscus

for

after another paradise puddles
the very sneer of chin stitches
frill perms frame enough form
tickered over long headlight
splash come forward nails
forked a flower an hour for supper
comeuppance chains in piece
flat arm sieved & arrows
seems suggest, forgets

marked for shame at stubhill
flew at an exit hum laughter urn
the sun scorned brightly grand
paired with perfume the breeze blew
hampered by weight, crawling
perseverance of were sundry cats
red star says "fish" leave the light on
dark off

blossoming lack for narrow
the blue is sky today
whole white
dash

From Yoke to Slacks

unstaged pretzel parellels, yoke
shirking the centre between jeans
fuzzed up and dogged down, yack
fleeced away shy organ leans
to which felting snapper, makes
shine one shelf louder whisper
tapped from A orange, pecks
of that kind of knowing internal
mood shouting discus, track
bounce dip disco bond to prep
unsolicited hide by barge, trick
chatter tied by intrusive raking
buoying up the corner, stacks
egginess sundown a rule rote
on stage ride engine, slacks

their native estuary

for Michèle Provost

it's been a day since michele
bent montreal in a photocopier
& waved back her gale black fan.

blasting with anarchy the dozing wheat ears;
charged fast blanketing white a mountain horizon;
paper airplanes spare changed fiddleless ply her wake.

transit sites crash trauma give up ancient dead &,
synchronicity it was samuel at the birch tree blue & alive,
when a packed rainbow arrived in new york, it bloomed claimless.

running the rage in the lip of a clown turning limpward in rain;
straddling a clipped coastline wearing intercontinental sleeves;
sky & sea, blunt indifference, reflected sun from windows, on chalk.

western cities boom on paper; stone & tape fasten lives like twins;
makers of cities burp, lasso & loosen garlanded cattle on freeways;
glad-handing plumbers set free new swimmers happily in their
native estuary.

local bats

on your balcony you said you'd been to Giza
& inside the pyramid of Khafra.
i said i climbed one of the pyramids.
& that in ancient times the sky would have been much darker.
still we were at twilight & you said you heard the local bats.

south

It's been a week since we bridged the living room
on foam plates circling around the ambient fizz
far from the bright island where they went south
to scorch a fuelled fan and I cant tell the phone
from the rose, not swollen but I rise slowly
from an incursion into water brought rain not thunder.
Now that autumn is here, there are clouds packed
in tight fisted hammers with hollow cores hung
in vacant corners waiting for a bird to break and sing.

a window up in four tercets

staring from the window
the fridge kisses me
we look together & shiver

& severed finger i cools
jogs sideways locks k
sudden sogginess blushes

crashmaster vs sock wallop
purring snok elastik qwop
chaise morrow clucky romp

all this from the window
the smiles & sneers imagine
floating up to our window

.bye !

.leaning on a doorhandle
left my girlfriend ' s , ah h
forgot my bro k e n glasses
at her thighs   :
drunken tourists !

which elephant e you were

w i s h i n g   y o u   w e r e   a n   e l e p h a n t
U wErE ElEpanned ErEi rEi
ErrabElla belle BALE ree ree ralE
fun E E E l l e e rr eeeeeeeeeee
R R ee eEEEEE e E E e
    e   e
we e   e
    e   e
were   e
 e   e
elephants   e
e   e   e
e   e
e   e
e   e
e   e
             e
              e

Some Little Songs

Monty Reid

Widely published as a poet and essayist, **Monty Reid** has produced a substantial volume of literary work. His volumes include *The Life of Ryley* (Saskatoon SK: Thistledown Press, 1981), *These Lawns* (Red Deer AB: Red Deer College Press, 1990), *The Alternate Guide* (Red Deer College Press, 1995), *Dog Sleeps* (Edmonton AB: NeWest Press, 1993) and *Flat Side* (Red Deer College Press, 1998), a collection of new and selected poems, *Crawlspace* (Toronto ON: House of Anansi, 1993), and the chapbooks *cuba A book* (Ottawa ON: above/ground press, 2005) and *Sweetheart of Mine* (Toronto ON: BookThug, 2006). His newest poetry collection, *Disappointment Island*, is part of the first season of books by Chaudiere Books. He has won the Stephan G. Stephansson Award for Poetry three times and is also a three-time Governor General's Award nominee. He spent nearly twenty years working at the Royal Tyrrell Museum of Palaeontology in Drumheller, Alberta, in the heart of the Alberta badlands, before moving to the Ottawa area in 1999 to work at the Canadian Museum of Nature.

Some Little Songs

(for skh)

i fridge

it has practiced
and now

it sings
when opened

open it
hold it open

those cherries
need to be eaten

ii furnace

bitter February night

less than half
a cold moon

rises over the canal
shaped like an ear

the furnace comes on

and stays on

iii bulb

she prefered
to make love

with a light on
somewhere

that's just
the way she was

the charged filament
pings ·

just slightly
where all those

excited particles
turn into light

iv doorbell

it was listening
to the frogs too much

and now it sounds
like them

no matter

when it asks
we let it in

v oscillating fan

come back

baby

come back

baby

come back

vi computer

there must be delicate
wiring
inside the box

what remains
outside the box

imagines itself

vii chair

it sings its song
to hold you

in this
it is not alone

viii floor

the weight of moonlight
passes

every night the hardwood
turns into something else

and then turns
back again

I know you heard something

but there's no one
there

ix pipe

it sings
reliably

every
morning

the girl
next door

steps in
the water

x moon

the moon
is burning
in the clouds

shadows
never know
their age

Obvious

At the moment, I think poetry
should be obvious. The little girl
in the restaurant had two short
pigtails. I took one in each hand
and said now I can feel exactly
what you're thinking.

No you can't, she said.

Sniffer Dog

I could be smuggling anything these days.
I had forgotten completely about the slice of Air Canada pizza
that was served just an hour before we landed, coming in from Brussels,
and since I wasn't hungry I just left it in its little cardboard box and
stuck it in my briefcase hoping to eat it later.

No such luck.
The perky little beagle they use for a sniffer dog at the Ottawa airport
trotted up to my luggage and barked at it, once
and delicately, and although I explained that it must be the pizza,
the guard just smiled and said please go through
that door over there.

Well, who'd be dumb enough to want Air Canada pizza
for later anyway? Quite a few it turns out.
When I pushed through the opaqued glass door I was at the end
of a line of about fifty people and over at the one open counter
there was already a stack of confiscated pizza containers
and they were calling in more help
to keep the line moving.

I did wonder for a moment
if it really was the pizza, and whether there was anything else
I had forgotten or if someone had stuck something
into one of my bags without me knowing
and god knows what was in them now.
That's what makes coming home so exciting, you
realize that you can't keep everything and sometimes
it takes a sniffer dog to remind you.

By the time I got to the counter it was routine.
I already had the pizza box out but they had to look
through things anyway and damn if they didn't find the little box of
Elisabeth chocolates I was bringing home for you. The ones with
dark chocolate drizzled onto fine slices of tangy orange.
They said it was fruit, and they took that too.

146

Shirts

There was a cool spring breeze
and she had washed his shirts
and hung them outside on hangers
in front of the window.

He was working at his desk
when he noticed movement
out of the corner of his eye.

First he thought someone
was coming to the door
and then he looked again
and those shirts made him feel

strangely empty, as if he
was out there blowing around
in the April wind.

Late in the afternoon
she gathered them in, pressing
them for a moment to her face,
taking in that crisp but

unmistakable smell
of no one.

Opening Night

It must have been a trick
of light. He was standing on the 2nd floor balcony
as the crowd gathered for the big flower show
on the main floor atrium. There would be
speeches.

He was scratching his beard
and flakes of dandruff were coming loose
cycling down in a column of light right onto the head
and shoulders of a balding man
from the embassy.

He noticed, smiled slightly to himself
and stopped, but dead skin takes its time
to fall. Beneath him, the man stood
attentively throughout the ceremony.
Only near the end did his wife
reach up to brush the shoulders
of his careful blue suit.

It wasn't til later, after all the speeches
were done and the warm sweet smell of
arranged flowers had secured the room
that the man on the balcony looked up
only now remembering
the two additional balconies
above him.

Old Wall

The backhoe hit it
when they were digging for the east parking lot
and of course the contractor didn't tell us
till he'd dug everything he thought needed to be dug

so when we went out to see it
there was a length of old wall exposed
about six feet under the current surface
with a gouge where the shovel went through it

and some chips of unwashed dishes stuck in the clay.
It's only a hundred years old, how could it get
so far down? The Earth must be contracting
that's my theory.

Hurry up, get some fill from somewhere
and cover this back up.

For a New Kitchen

(for Mary Ellen Herbert, September 23, 2005)

If you remember what the old kitchen
was like, shut up about it.

If you remember how the fat racoons
sat on the deck and complained

about the salad, or the silent moths
stopped at the screen, altho somehow

the light continued all the way in
and the old chairs that kissed

so much butt over the years
have gone back to their corners

knowing, always, they could be
the next to go, if you

remember any of that, just
zip it. They'll come back, or

something just like them will.
There is always a space

where the new world wants
to be made, there is always

a space that enters the old space
like a new image of our selves.

There are always this year's tomatoes
there on the granite counter

glowing.

Fixing the Goddess

The blessing goddess is broken.
Dropped somewhere en route
from Vancouver to Ottawa.
We thought she was packed safely
but when we opened the box
her head had broken off
and the thin clay of her breasts
was in a dozen pieces.
Somewhere along the line
we must have gotten careless.

We should have sent it
through the mail rather than
carry her with us. Maybe.
But she was a gift, and who knew
our trip would be so complicated?
No matter. We put her back
together, modestly, and reshaped
the missing pieces with drywall mud
and sanded everything down
smooth and put a waterproof
sealcoat on her.

She's ready to bless.

Now what do we do with her?

Moving the Dioramas

(for Christiane Saumur)

We are dismantling the illusion of nature.
That much beloved thing that generations
have stared at through the glass.
We need to move it to a new location.

We could put it anywhere, as long as
we can crate it up properly and the bigger pieces
fit through the window so the crane
can hook onto them.

Some people think they have made a great
discovery and announce there is nothing but illusion.
They should come and help us move the damn thing

We'll take the birds out one at a time
and do our best to conserve them. They're
full of arsenic and god knows what else.
But no dermestids that live on soft tissue and irony.

When it comes to the moose, well, we'll have to
put it in a sling and hoist it across the atrium.
We'll make it fly.

No one ever said it was anything but an illusion.
People loved it just the same.
They loved the fact that it was an illusion and they bumped
their noses on the glass looking for the goslings
in the bottom corner.

You can see the streaks.

Very Soon, And With Someone Pleasant

i

We waited for you for hours, in the small town chinese restaurant
where we always take visitors.

It was filling up on Friday night with all those appetites, for lemon
chicken, ginger fried beef, not too spicy please, because we are
eating out of hunger and no longer care what our bodies look like
and that just makes us
hungrier.

I know Don and Jan wanted to meet you and I kept making excuses
about the icy roads.

The tiny waitress, you know the one, kept asking if we were ready
to order and finally we told her to bring tea and appetizers
and then we couldn't wait any more. Sorry.

I don't remember what we had.
But I do remember breaking open the fortune cookies at the end
and mine said *very soon, and with someone pleasant.*

It was the same restaurant, and the menu hadn't changed much
either, except they added some Thai food. Bert and Don

had driven down from Edmonton in the first snowfall of the year
and had gotten lost. So they were late and I was worried
about the restaurant holding our reservation but when we arrived
there were lots of empty tables.

Don had a slab of rock with some old animal tracks in it
that he wanted someone to identify. He left them on the table
and the tiny waitress, she looks like she's about 12, carried them away
with the dishes.

She brought them back with the fortune cookies. Mine read *hard work
will be rewarded*. Bert explained that to get the most out of fortunes
you have to add the phrase *in bed* to the end of each.

Hard work will be rewarded, in bed. Etc.
I don't know where you were that time either.

iii

I picked Andrea up in Calgary so I know
the roads weren't too bad. They were expecting

us at the restaurant and were obviously disappointed
when you didn't show. This time you said
you were sick and since I got the same thing a week later

you probably were. Andrea had the hot and sour soup
and thought they put too much Worcestershire sauce in it.
I never knew that's what they used.

The tiny waitress, yes that one, brought the fortune cookies
along with the bill, which Andrea insisted on paying.
She wouldn't even let me look at it.

It's funny how the bill is such a private document
but our fortunes, even though each one is hand-delivered
as if it was meant for us and no one else, we look at them
and then we share them. So there's no
danger of believing them.

My fortune read *because of poetry your meal tonight is free*.
I should've saved it and shown it to you.

iv

What the body knows is never the body itself.
What it knows is only its own hunger, which acts as if
it had a life of its own. The tiny waitress was pregnant
and irritable and kept spilling the water.

Diana didn't particularly want to be there either. She was worried
the msg might give her a headache and she was planning on driving
all the way home the same night and they were calling for snow.

You would have liked her. She said
there were poets in the kitchen, deep in fish bones
and bok choy, and they made up the fortunes for everyone
that came through the doors, writing their eight-syllable poems
and slipping them inside their little nests of starch.
I saved an extra cookie for you

Or were you there that night?
My fortune read *when you are old you will eat alone.*

What I want to know, right now, is
once you have a fortune, can you send it back?

v

You were the one who taught me how to use chopsticks, sort of.
I still have a hard time with the noodles. The night Doug and Sharon
were there we all ended up wearing some of the oyster sauce.
I warned them about going home through Camrose
but they got a ticket anyway.

I don't care where you were. I don't care about the black ice
and the big trucks and all your other travelling anxieties.
Imagine trying to pick up Singapore noodles with a single stick.
That's how it makes me feel.

I was alone in the restaurant as the tiny waitress
cleared the tables. The cookie she had brought for you
sat untouched on the black raft of its tray, afloat
on all the grains and sauces of the evening.
I don't know what it said.

TENGO SED

Shane Rhodes

Shane Rhodes' first book, *The Wireless Room* (Edmonton AB: NeWest Press, 2000), won the Alberta Book Award. His second book, *Holding Pattern* (NeWest Press, 2002), won the Archibald Lampman Award. Shane is also featured in the anthologies *New Canadian Poetry* and *Breathing Fire II* and recently published a chapbook, Tango Sed, with Greenboathouse Books. His next book, *The Bindery*, is forthcoming from NeWest Press in 2007.

Caléndula

I write *marigolds in a clear vase* and hope by these words to contain it. By *it* I mean she had left three nights ago and now I miss her. She carries through my thought like the Spanish opera coming through my window: strangeness, missing and knowing song is no relief only the transition of a private worry to an unconjugated public domain.

The sea and its unending labour, the wind and its constant generalization of heat.

As if, in a revolution almost complete but before the final blow where the last city falls, the army of Mayan peasants were to put down their guns and return home to plant corn — for it is spring and unplanted seed shames the dirt. In a year, the peasants would be slaves again to the *mestizo* landowners and the dream of a homeland would fade to myth. As if I were to inhabit the suspended animation of that *as if*.

A fidelity beyond the reason I hear — the white pearl of moon, for instance, the coarseness of pubic hair to the touch.

Spring here and the fish market counters piled high with calico orange snapper, sky-grey grouper and sea bass. They lie on the counters, mouths agasp, glossy eyes turning creamy white as, one by one, the fishmonger scales them and fillets them alive.

Which surprised me the way the trays of fried shark meat surprised me when I saw them in the market beneath the picture of a seven-foot reefshark eating a human leg.

Like a 17th century still-life of fruit so ripe eating it would be a step down from an imagined taste or old morality plays in which one plays the beggar and another the glutton.

I have seen the dried blossoms of marigold strewn in geometric patterns around the graves. Dried, they cauterise wounds and guide the spirit home. Or, as Gerard says, they "cureth the trembling of the heart."

160

Their name in Spanish is *caléndula* from the Latin *calend* for the end of the month when they were thought to flower (like a woman) most strongly. But they make more sense to me in English as marigold, marsh gold, Mary's gold, the gold of the Virgin.

But switching languages does not get closer to what I mean, for, if anything, the change shows I do not know what I mean. I say *espero* from the Spanish verb *esperar* which means *to hope or to wish*

but which also means *to wait*.

Muerto de Hambre

The week before, her husband carried on his back from the market two 30 pound sacks of camotes or purple yams. On the day before the Day of the Dead, she cleans the camotes and, on a large charcoal fire in her outdoor kitchen, boils them until cooked. When cool, she peels and grinds them, or her daughters do, on the metate, a long grinding board and rolling pin hewn of volcanic rock. When the camote pulp is fine and paste-like, she puts it in a large copper kettle with water, sugar and colouring and boils it to a thick, pink paste. This work lasts all day and well into the night. Her face and the face of her daughters can be seen in the black stone kitchen fanning the fire which billows smoke. Their arms and faces dotted with pink miel de camote as it spits over the flame. No light except the light on their faces from the burning coals. It is hard work and, by the time they are done and all the pots and even some tea cups and mugs are filled with the camote, they are tired. But it must be made or the dead will go malnourished for the Day of the Dead is their only day back in this world. The family sets out food and treats (tobacco, tequila, salt) and dried flowers. The food is sugary but bland. Sugary for their spirits are like children and will only be attracted to the sweet. Bland for, somehow, the dead have already taken the flavour from it. And to commiserate with the dead, the family must also eat the sweet, bland food, which they do for the entire week after. Morning, noon and night they pile the special sweet white bread with mounds of camote and eat. They eat camote until they are full. They eat camote until they are tired. They try to give it away but instead are given more. They try to forget about it and when they forget about it, it is still on their plates. Every morning their bread piled high with camote and they eat. They eat until they are ready to die of it.

Tengo Sed

A Señora Ramona Lopez

To have aguamiel, it needs to be stored in a terra cotta cistern (*hecho de barro*) which will keep it cool (*frío*), and that cistern needs (*debe*) to be stopped with a rolled maguey leaf so it can breath (*respirar*) but not spill, and it all needs to be brought to town (*al pueblo*) on the back of a mule (*un burro*). But this stuff in plastic (*plástico*) jugs tied to a bicycle, she says (*me dice*), I wouldn't wash my dog (*lavar mi perro*) with it. When she was a child (*una niña*), every morning (*cada mañana*), she says, they would drink aguamiel (*tomábamos aguamiel*), a sweet greyish-green sap from the maguey cactus. It kept them healthy (*para nuestra salud*). With every meal her family would eat nopal (*nopales*), a thinner, leaf-like cactus cultivated on the sierra with chilli (*con chili*), tomato (*jitomate*), onion (*cebolla*), garlic (*ajo*) and a pinch of salt (*sal*). It kept us healthy. When the men wanted to get drunk (*emborracharse*), they drank (*tomaron*) pulque which was fermented aguamiel. When they wanted to get really drunk (*casi muertos*), they drank mescal which was something like (*un poco como*) pulque but distilled (*más fuerte*). But now she says, you cannot even buy the stuff (*no se puede comprarlo*). A boy (*hay un chico viene*) comes every morning (*cada mañana*) from the campo (*del campo*) with two four-litre plastic jugs of pulque and aguamiel tied to his bicycle. But this is not right (*pero, no está bien,*), she says (*me dice*).

The Market Place

I would buy the light that falls through the stained glass windows of these old churches.

> Flying into Mexico City from Merída, a long brown thread of smoke hangs over the crater of Popocatépetel.

I would join this economic union, here, at your hip.

> We took the same path as Cortez but 30,000 feet higher — in from the Gulf at what he named the Villa Rica de la Vera Cruz, then west through the mountain passes and plains. A passage replete with historical rhyme: foreign tankers full of Pemex crude and the stink of Conquistadors under full heat in full armour — soldiers whose only promise was looted gold while the ships to take it home were burned in the harbour.

I would market the shouts of these women who live in the street.

> The plane banks to the left and the passengers slump into their accumulated momentum. When the Spanish came to the volcano Popocatépetel in 1521, the Conquistador _____ was lowered into the crater with a bucket and a hammer; Indigenous guides above guiding the rope through the hot rocks. He came back to the surface with a pail full of sulphur – (he would die __ years later, in _____, destitute and _____)(this is history speaking) – to make gunpowder for the arquebus and cannon.

I would privatize this rain water puddle.

> Which gave them Tenochtitlan the first time.

I would sell this music coming through the cantina windows.

> Fleeing the city on the Noche Triste, many Conquistadors drowned in Largo Texcoco — unable to swim or float, their clothes so laden with gold.

I would steal this history.

> More buckets were lowered into the volcano, and the volcano ate them.

A Time of Gifts

We hiked all morning to get there. Up through
pine trees and jumbled scree, thick mattresses
of moss sucking at the summer storms.
At the top of the mountain ridge and to the north
a spooned-out hollow full to our feet
of blowing cloud, while, to the south, the sky
was clear and blank. And it seemed – walking
across that ridge – our feet slipping on shale
and mid-summer snow green with rock-dust –
we moved as light moves, on the constant
brink between two wholes incommensurate.
If you want something five times more distant,
said Leonardo, paint *it five times more blue.*

We descended in late afternoon, down through
the shrill screech of pika, high mountain meadows
with their last crescents of snow.
The hard religious hunger of rock-bound roots.
A feeling, then, of life bedded down deep
within itself. We had argued all day
and only now did a peace ascend to meet us
as the snowmelt flowed in an ermine-like lather
down through the valley below
where children filled with the rapture
of Guadalupe-Tonantzin appearing high
in the enamelled pine.
And when we returned to the city,
there were the signs and sounds cities make:
clink of cutlery, men on street corners
laughing and exchanging money.
Children played with summer-intensity
last games of tag. Everything still happened
for the first time.

Cuentas

They agreed, hiking the mountain which over-looked the city spires and silver mines, that their lives were already arthritic with worry.

On the mountaintop, they removed t-shirts, jeans and underwear to suntan — interrupted only by the goat herds eating brown grass dried tough by summer drought.

And they meant by "worry" an anxiety fed from its own imprecision and so became an italicised *sadness* — as in a life corroded by work, the lack of money, the loss of time.

With an afternoon rain shower, they dried themselves and descended, stopping only to pick cactus fruit – its cool skin and warm, lucent centre full of pits.

"This is how the middle-aged would live," he would say at times. "A life of pattern and routine with very little conscious waste."

And it makes me want a quick end to it: "They returned to their pension (the one with the beaten tile in every room), made dinner and turned out the lights" or "The grey/green pigeons, startled by the evening bells, flew from the gutters to the church spires".

Instead: in a restaurant that night, they ate green poblano chillies fried in batter and stuffed with meat, raisins and walnuts and topped with walnut nougat and pomegranate seeds.

A nun created the dish in 1826 to honour the ten-month despot rule of Augustin de Iturbide, self-claimed ruler of New Spain — deposed, exiled, returned, arrested, hung. hanged.

After, they drank coffee picked from mountains in Michoacán and brought up through Uruapan.

In its form, the restaurant mimicked Iglesia de San Cayetano below — built by a Spanish silver baron as thanks to the commercial graces of a saint rather than the indigenous slaves who worked the mines below.

But that is not all: the señora in Puerto Progresso said, looking from the government dock built for the luxury cruise ships to the surrounding mansions of the local rich, "Salinas was a crook! But he was lucky crook — the *cabrón* now lives in Ireland!"

A Note from Zacatecas

In the painting of Saint Francis in El Convento de Guadalupe just
outside of Zacatecas, the anonymous landscape is of an imagined
Europe — far off hills with tended sheep, oak forest, a small stream,
a dream of homeland. The colours of the painting are dark greens
and tar-oil blacks aged by the light and dry air as if to prove a
heaven should be composed only of light. The convent was built by
the Franciscans in the 19th century and called El Colegio Apostólica
de Propaganda Fide – the padres in their brown cowled shawls
sweating out their abeyances in the wind-kept deserts to the north.
By the 19th century, it would have been unclear for whom they were
apostlating. The light through the windows now is full of a blue
that will fill the streets with sleeping dogs. Bells continue to ring
from the high campanile for morning mass, linked by a long rope of
sisal to a padre in the plaza below. He pulls on the rope, gathering
what remains of the faithful.

La Fiesta de la Independencia de Santa Rosa

The main cobbled street filled with horses, men and women in costume. On one side, the Conservatives. On the other the Liberals. Or, the Spanish and the Mexicans. Or, those for the crown and those against it. On the Mexican uniforms, women have pinned small garlands of fruit and membrillos, a wild apple that grows in the surrounding hills. The air tinned with the smell of gunpowder. With a trumpet call, the Conservatives charge and the Liberals retreat. Dust and the exaggerated features of men playing fear. Then the action stops and the Liberals charge back. The sound of rushing horses and the exaggerated features of men playing victory. When the battle is finally over, a marching band of second-hand suits, trumpets and an old beaten tuba begins to play. A straw-stuffed general hangs from one corner of the stage. The vanquished dance with the victors. Men dance with men. Women dance with women. Someone dances with a dog. False moustaches and beards are ripped off as bottles of mescal pass from mouth to mouth, the rims shined with spit. Gunshots become less coordinated and more frequent. At the only cantina in town, a man, still on his horse, rides halfway through the door and asks for a bottle of beer. At the corner urinal and grinning at the horse, a man lets go a torrent of piss.

Unas Historias

In the evenings, I ran. The glabrous
skin of cactus in headlights. Dead dogs
wild with larva by the side of the road.
When it rained, water gathered
in small streams that turned to torrents
through the unnavigable streets. In the afternoons,
I avoided the heat and studied Mexican history.
You could walk half an hour from my
pension to the town granary where hung
the severed heads of the rebel leaders
a century before. When the Loyalists
retook the city, they held a 'lottery
of death' for they believed the townsfolk
too compliant. Each winner was tortured
and hung. *The violence of the body,*
says de Certeau, *reaches the page only*
through absence, through what is erased.
And maybe you'd say the same for pleasure.
They met his mother in Sweden where she'd moved
after escaping from Sudan. When she met
his white girlfriend, who he'd been
so proud to present, his mother said to him
later, privately, *Think of her as the kind of woman*
you meet on a train and with whom
you have a wonderful conversation
and, at the next stop, she gets off.
At night, we would hold each other tightly
and when we came our bodies shook
as the light in empty churches shakes
between the volcanic stone. It was chiselled
in the 16th century by indigenous labourers
each with a small raised brand on his cheek.

La Música

Two young men play guitar. They play in a small house where bare
light bulbs hang from the concrete ceiling. Outside it rains and
between breaks in the rain you can hear waves roaring to shore. We
are on the Gulf of Mexico and with each wave you can smell the
rancid breath of the sea, a mouth that has tasted and eaten
everything. One of the guitar players has a cell phone clipped to his
belt and behind him, on the wall, is a small shrine to the Virgin of
Guadalupe, her brown eyes lowered with all the beatific adoration
of an overdose. The men sing traditional songs — *pura yucateca* —
to an old man who sits on a blue stool before them. It is his birthday
and one of the boys playing guitar is his son who sings with a clear,
low voice and wears eyeglasses to look like John Lennon. The old
man has eyes that move with the semblance of sight. He has been
blind for 27 years and has never seen the son who plays before him.
The walls of the house are worn at the level of his hands. He sits
before the singers and around him are the people who have
gathered to celebrate his birthday. Somebody begins to dance and
they sing louder. There is food. There is beer. He is dying. They
sing old songs not to please the old man but because everybody
sings old songs. He mouths the words he knows and teaches the
singers new songs they don't know. He is another year older. He is
crying.

Carne

In a market in Mexico City, vendors sell tacos made from the meat of cooked goat heads. Beside the grills are piles of eyeless sockets and obstinate looking jaws still with their full array of stained teeth. You eat the meat from the head, a man tells me pointing at a skull while pushing a taco deep into his mouth, because then at least you know it's not rat meat.

La Brujería

Señor Lopez had a problem. His back hurt. Not just pain but a pain
that would not go away. Nothing would tempt it out of his muscles
and bones where it laid like a trodden upon snake. It hurt him
when he worked. It hurt him when he screwed. It hurt him when
he rested. His wife told him to go to the woman who lived on the
edge of the campo. He went to her and said, I think somebody has
put a curse on me. She said, let me see, and dealt him his cards.
Somebody has put a curse on you, she said. To rid yourself of the
curse, make a tea from these herbs and drink it for a week. At the
end of the week, kill a chicken and sprinkle its blood on the ground
outside your door, then throw the chicken away. Señor Lopez
thanked her many times — always leave on good terms with your
bruja, your witch — and went away. Señor Lopez drank the tea.
Señor Lopez killed the chicken and — when no one was looking —
sprinkled its blood outside his door. When he was done, he threw
the chicken away. Señor Lopez' back is fine again.

La Dueña

The wind blew at just under 300 kilometres per hour. Even on the
shallow shore, the waves and tide swell had reached 13 feet. When
the family returned to their house after waiting out the hurricane
further inland, there was nothing left. The waves had entered and
left each room and taken everything with it. Doors, television, gas
stove, fridge, curtains, carpets, stamps, forks, spoons, pictures. The
only thing left behind was beach sand which had piled up the walls
to the rafters. Even fifteen years after the hurricane, everyone still
keeps their important pictures and letters in small sacks hung at the
end of their beds so they can be grabbed quickly. The family buys
nothing that can't be easily left behind. They work as landlords in
the town, renting summer houses to winter foreigners like me. But,
she says, this Yucateca woman in her sixties who still remembers
living with her mother in a small Mayan cabaña with dirt floors, the
sea is our landlord, our dueña.

In the Cantina Las Americas

Women dance around men
      who are also dancing in a way —
          this corner
that corner
          sidestep
      justice
the anointed bones.
      The bartender
          at the back of the bar
is cool
      and barely awake.
          He pours tequila
into shot glasses
      the amber colour
          of palm oil.
Already the day is full:
      the despot general
          paraded his amputated leg
through the streets
      while the American bureaucrats
          – appalled –
applaud
      oaths
          sanitary adjectives
trainloads of armaments
      and the rustle
of assassins in the woods.
      Light shimmers
          from disco balls
that remember nothing
      to the man in the corner
          grinding
against his partner's torso.
      He must be Economic Liberalization
          and she the Working Poor.
No, he's the World Bank
      and she Monetary Transcendence
and Devaluation.
      But you are a tourist here —
          you look
and look away.

On Travel

For anyone who has been sung to in Hebrew by a naked Israeli at 2
     in the morning.

For the girl learning Spanish from English who only spoke Japanese.

For there are boys in Orissa playing cricket with the sea.

For the seventy caged birds at the small pension in which we stayed
     that, every morning, woke us with song.

For the Amritisar-Howrah-Amritsar Mail and our 20 hours thereon,
     thereon, thereon.

For the man on a street corner selling his amazing invention that
     kills rats and cockroaches for only 6 pesos.

For only 6 pesos.

For, in Mexican Spanish, "me late" means I like it, or, literally, it
     makes my heart beat.

For only that which goes on hurting will be remembered.

For the man who said I looked like George Michael and then sang
     "Careless Whisper" stopping, at appropriate pauses, for my
     approval.

For yak cheese hung out to dry in the wind.

For the only way to kill a cockroach, I have found, is to tell it stories
     of depravity.

For, when you have everything and nothing, it's only the nothing
     that hurts.

For the Mexican bus driver who stopped in the middle of a busy
     street and, with an array of honks and complicated hand
     gestures, made a date with the woman working cash at a
     convenience store.

For those who make love in overnight buses thinking the other
     passengers do not hear.

For the temple baboons threatening the faithful with their angry red
     asses.

For it is so still in this room / even the razors sleep.

For the sound of a spider chasing a cricket across a marble floor.

For, here, Castles become Elephants and Queens merely Advisors.

For there are prayer flags even the wind can't read.

For I am as still, tonight, as Pascal sitting in an empty room.

For the old women in the market selling fried grasshoppers from the
     pockets of their aprons.

For high up in the Himalayas / you open the door / the clouds
     come in.

For the village family who named their son Usmail after an
envelope carrying the stamps of a foreign country.

"Buenos Aires

es como un plano / de mis humiliaciones y fracasos" – I read from a copy of Borges I bought in a tienda for 20 pesos.

My hostel room on Hipólito Yrigoyen just down from Plaza de Mayo is cheap because it's beside a porn cinema. All day and night, street noises mix with the long lingering polyglot moans of faked female orgasm.

In 1946, Perón appointed Borges the "Inspector of Poultry and Rabbits in the Public Markets," as an insult.

Three decades later, Borges was appointed director of the Biblioteca Nacional, which was built on the razed deathbed home of Eva Perón as an insult.

More surprising than the sexthrob vibrating through the hostel wall is the intermittent sound of German dialogue and racecars.

This city is like a library to me, its streets a plan of humiliations and failure.

In the square before the presidential palace, grandmothers tie white bandanas on the trees or carry pictures of their children to remember how the government tortured them and threw the bodies to the sea.

"In endeavouring to describe these scenes of violence, one is tempted to pass from one simile to another," wrote Darwin in his journal in 1834 while hiking through the Pampas.

As he grew older and blind, Borges wrote more poetry (for he could carry poems in his head) and paid young men to read to him.

Two men in a room — one reading stories he has never before seen; one listening to the stories he knows but cannot read.

Is this history?

When he was old, a writer from Argentina says on the radio, recounting the literati before and after the coup, *Borges became a fool, believing what other people told him, shaking hands with Pinochet.*

To Elizabeth Bishop

Here is a coast. Here is a harbour.
Here is beach sand. Here is owned land.
Here is an economist. Here is a fine mist.
Here is a dock. Here is a flock of birds.
Here is a trade. Here is a woman in labour.
Here is trade. Here is a woman's labour.
Here is a border zone. Here is a pay phone.
Here is free trade. Here is a man getting paid.
Here is a market place. Here is its church.
Here is its steeple. Here is nada para amor.
Here is a calle. Here is a detalle.
Here is a mercado. Here is a SuperMercado.
Here is a Zapatista. Here is a Pípila.
Here is a revolucionario. Here is a federalista.
Here is a trabajador. Here is your zapato.
Here is 200 murdered women.
Here is a fábrica. Here is some maquillaje.
Here is a turista. Here is an assembly line.
Here is an assembled line. Here is the blazing divine.
Here is a smokestack. Here is a wire rack.
Here is product X purchased at £100.
Here is a statue to commemorate. Here is a statute to commiserate.
Here is the policía. Here is the beautiful song.
Here is the beautiful song. Here is the beautiful song.
Here is a room. Here is a man sitting.
Here is his hammock. Here is his beach sand.
Here is his coast. Here is his harbour.

Acknowledgments:

Stephen Brockwell:
"Bill McGillivray's Cap" appeared in *The Danforth Review*
"Hammer" and "The Last Eloquence of Uncle John" appeared in *Yawp*
"Sorus" appeared in the chapbook *O Helios!* from the Olive reading series
"Ingredients for Certain Poems by Al Purdy" appeared in an above/ground press chapbook as part of *The Ivory Thought* a University of Ottawa conference on Al Purdy.

Anita Dolman:
"The offer" and "Subconscious" appeared on *Latchkey.net* in October 2005. "Blindness" and "Fishing" appeared in *The Antigonish Review*, 141/142. "After" appeared on *the punk rock poet's blog* in May 2005, while "Chase" was published in *ottawater.com*, No. 0.1. "Shoes" was published as broadside #175 (Ottawa ON: above/ground press, 2003), and also appeared in *Grain Magazine,* Vol. 31, No. 1. Several of the poems included also appeared in the chapbook *Scalpel, tea and shot glass* (Ottawa ON: above/ground press, 2004).

I would also like to thank, as always, my husband, James Moran, for his unwavering support and encouragement.

Anne Le Dressay:
Some of these poems have previously appeared in *Arc*, *Prairie Journal*, and *The New Quarterly*, or online at *ottawater.com*.

Karen Massey:
"Photograph", "Cold Water Wash", "Winter Afternoon Zen", "Not a Sonnet" originally appeared online in *Ottawater 2*.

Una McDonnell:
Some of these poems originally appeared in *Arc magazine*, and in *Musings: An Anthology of Greek Canadian Literature*, Vehicule Press, eds. Tess Fragoulis, Helen Tsiriotakis, Steven Heighton, 2004. "The Heart's Dumb Memoir" appeared recently in *Rampike*.

rob mclennan:
"bicycle music" originally appeared as above/ground press broadside #254, published for a weekend including The League of Canadian Poets' Annual General Meeting, Ottawa, June 9-12.

Max Middle:
Versions of the following previously published:
"an i or an I" *1 Cent* #363
"dear jc" above/ground press broadside #207, *Shift & Switch: New Canadian Poetry* (Mercury Press, 2005)
".bye !" *Peter F. Yacht Club*, Issue #4
"an MMSP C Poem" above/ground press broadside #231
"Petty Crime" *Peter F. Yacht Club* #2
"local bats" *smthg* (above/ground press, 2005)
"b being still" *Ottawater* #1, *smthg* (above/ground press, 2005)
"lace" *flow march n powder blossom s* (above/ground press, 2006)
"C" *two by two on that oversized lifeboat, Peter F. Yacht Club*, 2005
"run scrummee" *Peter F. Yacht Club*, Issue #4, *flow march n powder blossom s* (above/ground press, 2006)
"zedders" *flow march n powder blossom s* (above/ground press, 2006)
"a gleaner" *flow march n powder blossom s* (above/ground press, 2006)
"a kickstand down in five tercets" *flow march n powder blossom s* (above/ground press, 2006)
"is never the never R u there" *flow march n powder blossom s* (above/ground press, 2006)
"From Yoke to Slacks" *Peter F. Yacht Club*, Issue #2, *smthg* (above/ground press, 2005)
"A Text for One Voice" *Murderous Signs* #11
"The New Wolves" above/ground press broadside #188, ImPress leaflet (2005)
"their native estuary" *Peter F. Yacht Club* #5
"feet, steps" *Peter F. Yacht Club* #5
"Some Jewelry" *Incunabula: graduate journal of arts and literature, smthg* (above/ground press, 2005)
"south" *flow march n powder blossom s* (above/ground press, 2006)

Monty Reid:
"Moving the Dioramas" poem first appeared in *Arc*.
"Some Little Songs" appeared first in *Disappointment Island*. (Chaudiere Books, 2006)
"For a New Kitchen" first appeared as a broadside from Sidereal Press in 2005.
"Very Soon, and With Someone Pleasant" first appeared in *Querty*, and was reprinted in *Disappointment Island*. (Chaudiere Books, 2006)

Shane Rhodes:
Earlier versions of these poems were published in *West Coast Line, Ottawater, filling Station, The Fiddlehead*, and *Arc*. I would like to thank the editors. As well, many of these poems were published in a limited edition chapbook entitled

Tengo Sed -- and designed by Jason Dewinetz of Greenboathouse Books –
which won second place in the limited edition category at the Alcuin Society
23rd Annual Awards for Excellence in Book Design in Canada.

About the cover artist:

Bhat Boy was born in England in the 1960s. As a child he became a naturalized Canadian and grew up in Canada's National Capital with his parents - a cleaning lady and a spy.

Known for his colourful work and imagination, Bhat Boy spends much of his time traveling about with his paintings, selling work in Canada, the United States and Europe. He has had shows in Florence, Toronto, San Francisco, London and Ottawa. His work can be found on every continent but Antarctica.

His work can be found at www.bhatboy.com